SUCCESSFUL SELLING WITH NLP

This book gives you the method and power to manage *you!*

Steve Fagan
Vice President, European Operations, Compuware Ltd

One of the many good things about this book is how it really links a value based approach to practical common sense action.

The importance of ethical business is recognised, yet often seen as an unaffordable luxury in the hard world of commerce. By linking a value driven approach to common sense action, this book shows it is not a luxury but a practical necessity.

Derek Pierce
Chief Executive of Leeds Training and Enterprise Council

Joseph O'Connor and Robin Prior have given us an entertaining, relevant and immediately applicable guide to solving sales problems with the power of NLP.

Lara Ewing
NLP trainer

D0474946

SUCCESSFUL SELLING WITH NLP

THE WAY FORWARD IN THE NEW BAZAAR

Joseph O'Connor
and Robin Prior

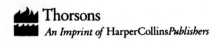 Thorsons
An Imprint of HarperCollins*Publishers*

Thorsons
An Imprint of HarperCollins*Publishers*
77–85 Fulham Palace Road
Hammersmith, London W6 8JB
1160 Battery Street
San Francisco, California 94111–1213

Published by Thorsons 1995
10 9 8 7 6 5

Joseph O'Connor and Robin Prior assert the moral right to
be identified as the authors of this work

A catalogue record for this book
is available from the British Library

ISBN 0 7225 2978 3

Printed and bound in Great Britain by
Creative Print and Design Wales, Ebbw Vale

CONTENTS

FOREWORD

A great deal of management time is currently devoted to the 'new' consumer. This mythological creature buys, he isn't sold to. He has developed, overnight, a critical thinking process designed to shame Victor Kiam back to wet shaving. Strategic planning departments across the nation are replacing salesmen with computer purchasing systems and/or clerks. There is a quasi-religious fervour attached to various regulating bodies, seemingly aimed at putting salesmen in their perceived rightful place – the history book!

As this thought-provoking book points out, selling is an honourable profession and the most improbable profession to pursue without self-esteem. It both provides personal gratification to customers and enables them to protect the lives of their families. It is only debased by companies who offer poor products and even worse leadership and management. There are indeed no bad soldiers, only bad officers.

Neuro-linguistic programming, or NLP, provides us with a frame-work. A framework to recognise important things within ourselves and the way we relate to others. It offers great potential to thinking organisations who offer value for money products with sustainable remuneration and recognition systems. It is for the listeners and learners, not the sandbaggers. I have used it at TSB and it works.

Perhaps the greatest crime we vest on selling is to regard it as a stand alone process. It isn't. To borrow liberally from Churchill, it can and should only represent the end of the beginning. A business colleague recently told me of a sign that hung in his local butcher's shop: 'Service is our salesman.' Alliterative maybe, but I couldn't put it better than that.

The new bazaar referred to in the book must carry a similar promise. The old bazaar, vocal in the extreme, cannot.

Geoffrey Gray

Geoffrey Gray is a Regional Director of TSB plc. He has been associated with the selling of financial services for 25 years.

PREFACE

The problem I see with most sales training is all the stress it puts on 'closing the sale'. Instead, I believe the stress should be put on *opening the relationship*.

Salesmanship is a very empty activity if all it is concerned with is making a fast buck, irrespective of what the customer's real needs are. That kind of shallow approach is in the long run self-defeating as a way of earning a living and certainly offers little in the way of a satisfying career.

But if salespeople take a longer view, and approach their task from the viewpoint of identifying and meeting customer needs, then their way is opened to a life that is not only more interesting and exciting but also more rewarding as well. Because the person who nurtures customer relationships by responding to their needs is building an income stream that will continue to grow over many years.

One of the reasons why I enjoyed this book, and why I think it will be useful to anyone engaged in any kind of selling (even if it is only selling yourself), is because of the strong emphasis that Joseph O'Connor and Robin Prior put on building a relationship with customers. Building relationships is what successful selling and successful marketing are all about.

However, it is not enough just to aspire to being a relationship builder: as with anything else, you have to work at the techniques that will deliver what you want. Neuro-Linguistic Programming is a valuable new tool in this area, if you can get beyond the obstacle of that horrible name!

This book clearly shows how NLP principles can be applied to the selling situation, to the mutual benefit of both buyer and seller – and that can't be bad.

Feargal Quinn

Founder of the Irish supermarket group Superquinn and author of *Crowning the Customer*

ACKNOWLEDGEMENTS

Many people have helped us with this book.

Thank you to Ian McDermott of International Teaching Seminars for your support and ideas, especially in the sales management section.

Thank you, Mike Kearsley, for your involvement and constructive input throughout the project.

Thank you, Bob Janes, Geoff Avis and Dave Watkins, for reading an initial draft and giving very constructive and useful feedback.

Thank you, Steven Robbins, for many interesting ideas and discussions on Compuserve. Good luck in your endeavours.

Thanks to Mick Rennie for many stimulating discussions on selling after our games of squash.

Thank you, Nick Rennie and Laurie Rambaud, for your support and enthusiasm.

To our editors at Thorsons, Elizabeth Puttick and Elizabeth Hutchins, thank you for your work.

And finally, many thanks to David Gaster who, before his untimely death, was a help and inspiration to us both. His work on leadership and the model of congruence that he projected were a major influence on the content and style of this book.

We gratefully acknowledge all the help we have had with this book and the end result is our responsibility.

Joseph O'Connor
Robin Prior
June 1994

INTRODUCTION

It is a black, brittle, cold morning. No sound comes to break the ice of the new day. You open one eye and stare at the luminous hands on the clock. There is an hour to go before you need to get up. Should you go back to sleep? Should you make use of this additional waking time, have that extra cup of tea, drive more safely, prepare for the meeting? There is a long journey to your first appointment. And you need another sale this month. The pressure is on. Management are showing signs of panic. Panic normally precedes the search for scapegoats. Today's sale would make you safe. The commission from it would pay some outstanding bills. And the bed is warm. You wonder, could you have worked harder at school, achieved more qualifications? Could you have been a solicitor, a doctor or a television presenter?

In your mind's eye you can picture ice formed on the windscreen of your car. And the bed is warm. You leap out of bed and shout, 'Hooray! Another day selling. Wonderful! I would rather be in sales than anything else in the world.'

Or perhaps:

You wake to find your thoughts full of everything you need to sort out when you get to the office. Gone are the days of that half-sleeping, half-waking state. From the second your eyes open, your brain is working on problems. Senior management are pushing for results. You, in turn, have pushed your salespeople. But they say the market is changing, it's not possible to meet targets with the economy as it is. You have fed this message upwards to the Sales Director but he won't accept it. He can't. If figures aren't met, the company is in trouble. You have to get blood out of a stone. And if you don't? It could be your neck on the line – and you didn't set the targets. You cannot possibly afford to lose your job – how could you meet your family commitments? You might have to find a scapegoat to show that you are trying, doing something. How about sacking someone to buy a bit of time? How would they feel about that? They didn't set the targets either. Nobody said business had be fair. You leap out of bed and shout, 'Hooray, isn't sales management wonderful?'

If this is your greeting to every day then put this book down because you do not need it. You can write your own. If you are still reading then we have something in common. We both know that selling can build you up and knock you down. It can be wonderful one day and tough and draining the next.

We all influence people. This is 'selling'. And the better we are at 'selling', the more we are likely to achieve what we want to achieve. Yet despite the fact that all of us 'sell' something – products, services, ideas, ourselves (although we do not always like to call it selling), selling has a poor public image. Many people, even senior managers in our own companies, look on salespeople as being manipulative and not quite normal, even though they would admit that sales is the life blood of the business.

Selling is not an easy profession. And the common opinions and assumptions about it make it harder than it need be. Over time, your enthusiasm and commitment may be worn down by constant negative messages about selling and salespeople. This is why there are so many sales books, training courses and consultancies dealing with the motivation of salespeople, and why inspirational sales speakers pack sports stadia for their seminars.

But long-lasting motivation does not come from shouting positive thoughts at the mirror or from shunning negative thoughts. Long-term motivation comes from clarity or purpose, clear objectives and a sense of doing something valuable. These we hope to give you.

This book is for salespeople, sales managers and sales trainers who want to look at the selling profession from another angle and to add further skills to those they already have. It is also for professional advisers, accountants and consultants who have to sell their services yet do not think of themselves as salespeople.

What is this 'other angle', this other way of looking at selling? It is the way you can define the word 'success'.

Much of this book applies the skills of Neuro-Linguistic Programming, or NLP, to the process of selling. It is not an NLP course and assumes no prior knowledge of NLP. NLP was developed originally by John Grinder and Richard Bandler in the mid-1970s. There are now national associations of NLP in countries all over the world, and it is widely used in business, education, training, therapy and sports performance.

NLP deals with influence: how people relate and communicate to others, how they make decisions and how they prefer to be influenced, so it is particularly useful in selling. The skills of NLP fit well in a world putting greater emphasis on quality, customer care and sales accountability.

NLP also enables us to study or 'model' what makes our top performers better than our average performers. By modelling these differences we can teach everyone in our sales team to benefit from the methods of our 'high fliers'. Modelling is part of that elusive Holy Grail of the sales profession: to discover the qualities of good sales-people, to be able to train others in those qualities and to select them in recruitment.

This is a practical book. It is designed to be used as a workbook. However, we do not make outlandish claims for it. You may not double your sales volume in three weeks. But if you apply and prac-tise the skills we cover, you will make a difference to your personal and professional life. Although there are anecdotes, stories and examples throughout the book to reinforce what can be achieved with NLP, the most compelling evidence will be your own experience.

This book is not only about selling skills, but also about taking care of your own health and well-being, about realising what is important to you and increasing the satisfaction you get from your life and work. There are many people who are overtly successful, making good money, yet feel unhappy. There are also many salespeople who feel pressured: they *have* to be the top performer, they *must* be a super sales ace, for anything less is failure. Some sales books and trainings, too, imply that aiming at anything less than perfection is second rate, losing, and if you do not make it to the top there must be something lacking in you. But not everyone wants to be top of the ladder if reaching such heights means unacceptable sacrifices in other parts of their life. We hope to help you find the balance that works for you – and your company – so that you can define your own measurement of success. It may even be in another profession.

We also cover the skills needed by a good sales manager: how to create an organisation where salespeople will give their best; how to be a leader and not a slave driver.

We came to write this book from our combined experience of many years in sales training, consulting and NLP. We saw the need for a book that not only dealt with the skills needed to succeed in selling, but also with creating a good self-image and public image of the profession where those skills can flourish.

There is a series of practical exercises interspersed throughout the book and more in a special section at the back. These exercises form the basis of a sales training that we conduct for sales organisations throughout the country. It is amazing that while there are many professional qualifications in marketing, there are none at the time of writing for salespeople.

Depending on your experience, training and prior reading, you may find some parts of this book cover familiar ground. This review of the known is deliberate, on the basis that if you are going to jump into new territory, you need firm ground to jump from. Also, no book could match perfectly the needs of every reader, because every reader has different needs. You all have different starting-points and different destinations.

Unfortunately, the English language has not kept pace with modern thinking. There is no singular, neutral pronoun. In writing this book, we have used 'he' or 'she' in alternate sections to reflect that sales-people and customers may be male or female, and to avoid awkward phrasing.

We have included a glossary of terms at the end but trust that we introduce words and phrases in a way that makes their meaning clear.

You are our customer. We aim to give you the skills that will enable you to sell more, if that is what you want, and to achieve the balance you choose between your professional and personal life. Whatever you sell, and whatever your level of experience, we hope you enjoy this book, find it useful and practical, and use it to get what you want from this fascinating profession.

Joseph O'Connor
Robin Prior
June 1994

How to use this book

This book is best read in sequence, but you can jump from section to section, and also within sections, depending on your interests. There are ideas and exercises throughout. The series of practical exercises in Part 5 is the core of the book (see pp.189–205). Do these exercises, as well as reading the book, if you want to make a difference to your sales skills.

PART ONE

HOW SELLING IS CHANGING

THE OLD BAZAAR

A politician, architect, surgeon and a salesperson were having a discussion about whose profession was the oldest.

'Well,' said the surgeon, 'God made Eve from Adam's rib – a surgical job, surely?'

'Ah,' replied the architect, 'before that, God created order out of chaos, and that is work for an architect.'

The politician made what he thought was the *coup de grâce*. 'And who do you think created the chaos originally?'

Then they all looked to the salesperson for his contribution.

'And who persuaded God that the whole project was a good idea in the first place?'

All professions have a public image and selling has a poor one. Yet selling is helping people get what they want, isn't it? Not to many people. To them the word 'selling' conjures up negative images and feelings. Stereotypes such as the used car salesman willing to say anything to sell a car come readily to mind. The film 'Tin Men' starring Danny de Vito is about salesmen selling aluminium house cladding in America. Operating in pairs, they work a scam. One sells the product at a ridiculously low price to the householders. A little later his partner calls, apologises and explains that the first salesman is having a nervous breakdown. He then asks the customers to pay the real price and not ruin the salesman's life, which they do.

Viewing selling as manipulating people to buy products or services they do not want is taken to its logical conclusion by a friend of mine. He believes that selling and advertising are the arts of arresting a person's intelligence for long enough to get money from them. If someone tries to sell him something, he automatically thinks it is no good, otherwise they would not be trying to persuade him to buy it. He decides what he wants and then goes and buys it. He is hardly ever open to external influence, because he assumes salespeople will attempt to deceive him.

When customers carry these negative beliefs about salespeople, and treat you as if you do not care what they want or are a necessary evil, it not only makes selling a difficult task but also reduces your sense of self-worth. When people expect you to act in a certain way you may become drawn to do so. When they expect you to be unethical it becomes easy to meet their expectation.

The word 'selling' encourages this poor image. It is important to remember that selling is only one half of the story. You cannot have a seller without a buyer. By forgetting the buyer, selling becomes misrepresented as a one-way influence, whereas a sale is the result of co-operation and interaction between the two. Thinking about selling as something done *to* customers instead of something done *with* customers distorts what is taking place.

Many sales books inadvertently reinforce this negative view of selling. They use metaphors like (and we quote), '...you apply the appropriate sales pressure with the appropriate drill bits (the selling skills), to enable you to bore through even the toughest of woods, the customer.' We suggest boring the customer is not a useful metaphor. Nor do I, as a customer, want to be compared to a block of wood.

Other books use war metaphors. Selling is defined as a 'skilled battle' fought by the salesperson. The enemy is your customer. And you then become the customer's enemy. Customers and clients may react by treating salespeople badly and wanting something for nothing.

War metaphors mean that you need new, sophisticated weaponry in your selling arsenal, so sales books become arms catalogues. Buying into this metaphor will give you combat fatigue. There are books of the 'hard closing' school that tell you that you have to drag the customer to the altar or land him like a fish. Other books give the message that selling is so difficult that you need to hypnotise yourself *and* the customer to be successful. Acting from these views of selling is bound to create resistant customers. Sales resistance is the triumph of mind over patter.

When selling becomes difficult then your motivation and enthusiasm wane. The more customers treat you badly, the less you are likely to care about them. When customers become difficult you might think the answer is yet more of the latest red hot sales tips to really get that sale. While these can be useful, they do not answer the basic problem and are rather like the Light Brigade sharpening their sabres as they

charge towards the Turkish guns. The more you rely on external motivation, the less you use your own resources. The voice in your head may try to bully you into feeling more enthusiastic: 'I should feel motivated. What's wrong with me?' Yet motivation that makes a difference can only come from the *inside*.

It is not easy to be motivated in this old-fashioned sales climate, for it is not a comfortable place to be. There have been surveys carried out where salespeople have been asked for the first thought that comes into their head in response to the word 'selling'. The results are interesting. 'Anxiety', 'resistance', 'stress' and 'loneliness' all appear. Also, because of the public image of salespeople, professionals such as accountants are uncomfortable about the thought of 'selling' their services. Selling is beneath them, something that not very nice people do. It is like putting themselves up for judgement and rejection.

Selling in this climate needs two qualities. One is called 'ego drive': how much you really want to make the sale. The second is called 'ego strength': how much you can withstand rejection. On these two measures, some surveys conclude that up to 80 per cent of salespeople are unsuited to the profession.

We are calling this model of selling the 'Old Bazaar' – where selling is thought of as one-way influence and salespeople are increasingly driven to sell to increasingly reluctant customers by whatever means they can. The salesperson has to force himself to sell and force the customer to want the product. It is the battle of the fittest, where there is no place for conscience. Buyer beware!

The cost of the Old Bazaar

The unfortunate consequences of the Old Bazaar are becoming more visible, not only for salespeople and customers, but also for companies and whole industries.

The insurance industry in particular is being transformed. As we write, legal cases are being fought over financial advice given by insurance companies on pension plans. A number of people were persuaded to change from company pensions to private pensions, a move that turned out to their financial disadvantage. The companies that gave this advice are being held responsible and are liable to pay compensation. There is no allegation that the insurance salespeople deliberately misled the customers (although there are many within the industry who would secretly admit that bad practice was encouraged, even from the highest levels), but the advice was mistaken and the company is liable. This is a result of new legislation that made the insurance salesperson or his parent company more clearly liable for the consequences of his actions. Now, some companies have their senior managers scrutinise every new policy sold by their sales force. If the manager has any doubt whatsoever that the policy suits the customer's domestic and financial circumstances, he will cancel it, *even if the customer protests.*

In 1994 Norwich Union was fined £300,000 plus £25,000 costs by the Life Assurance and Unit Trust Regulatory Organisation (Lautro) for failing to train its staff to the required Lautro standard. Norwich Union suspended all of its 800 salespeople for retraining to full Lautro standard, with full compensation offered to any investor who was found to have been given unsuitable advice. Mr Donald Dewar, the Labour Party social security spokesman, said, '...the extraordinary events at Norwich Union were startling evidence of the problems which had undermined confidence in selling methods and standards in the private pensions sector.'

This debacle in the private pensions sector has raised more worrying questions about the life assurance industry. Will the savings products that people have been encouraged to invest in since April

1984 ever meet their expectations? Has life assurance been eroded by poor product design, high charges and lax regulation? Criticism of personal pensions and the way they have been sold can be applied equally to most investment-linked products the insurance industry has been selling.

Under the Financial Services Act, insurance salespeople employed by, or tied to, an individual insurance company may not recommend the products of another company. This almost always leads to them selling one of their own policies. However, best pooled investments are likely to be where costs are lowest. The reason the costs are lowest is because they do not pay commissions and costs to insurance sales-people. They are therefore not recommended by salespeople! So in this case the structure of sales actually works against the customer.

There is further bad news. A survey of 18 companies by the Life Insurance Marketing and Research Association (Limra) found 42 per cent of salespeople left their company in 1992. Projecting these figures means that almost 80 per cent of life assurance salespeople leave their companies within two years of joining and only 8 per cent will have been with their companies for four years. This has hardly improved on the 1964 figures, where the turnover was approximately 50 per cent in the first year and 89 per cent in the first three years. Little has changed in 30 years. There is a vast cost here: wasted salaries and training, company time and reputation, and permanently burned territory. Enough is enough.

Also, there seems to be a strong correlation between staff turnover and policy lapse rates. A report by AKG, a firm of actuarial consul-tants, based on the latest set of the Department of Trade and Industry returns, suggests that the number of investment-linked life assurance policies that are cancelled early is high and rising. Nearly a quarter of all policies sold in 1991 were cancelled within a year, as customers realised they did not want them after all. Fewer than 70 per cent of policies survived 2 years. Overall, this means huge losses for investors through surrender penalties. Policies sold through independent financial advisers are 20 per cent less likely to lapse than plans sold by company salesmen. The insurance industry is the most graphic example of how the Old Bazaar affects us all.

One further example of the Old Bazaar comes from the photocopier industry, which is trying to increase control over members and agents to improve practices after sharp criticism of sales methods from the Office of Fair Trading. Codes of practice are being tightened to provide greater protection for customers – one particular instance being contract terms which extend beyond the life of the equipment and steep penalties for cancellation. In an ironic twist, some photo-copier salespeople dismissed for dishonest practice are offering to help customers unwind difficult contracts and exploit loopholes in the fine print. How successful will they be at selling their services?

These are two of the most visible examples of current changes, but the consequences of the Old Bazaar are not confined to these two industries. For the customer, the results are poor sales advice, products and services that do not meet needs. This breeds dissatisfied customers who make their next purchase at another company and become cynical about salespeople. For the organisation, it creates dissatisfied salespeople who are constantly moving on. The cost of hiring and training good salespeople is very large, especially in the insurance industry where policies are complex and well trained agents are needed to explain their labyrinthian ways. There is a high business cost to the old selling methods in the Old Bazaar.

THE ELECTRONIC BAZAAR

In the last few years, high technology has taken many jobs from people. It is now presenting companies with another way of selling their products other than using salespeople. This trend is the Electronic Bazaar. It is here now and its remorseless advance is fuelled by three main factors. First, the need to stop the manipulative prac-tices of the Old Bazaar. It is the nemesis of the old ways. Secondly, it is usually more cost-effective; technology is cheaper than labour. Thirdly, it is easy. Technology becomes more sophisticated every month.

Here are a few examples of the Electronic Bazaar. Banks are using computers to assess whether or not customers should receive a loan; it is believed that computers make fewer mistakes. The bank managers who presided over the automation of banking services in the 1980s now find that their own work is being automated. The financial services sector is currently trying to de-skill the role filled at the moment by the financial services adviser (insurance salesperson as was), believing that, again, the computer is more accurate with its advice. There are systems in use that give almost complete control to the customer. The customer enters details of income and expenditure, wants and expectations, and the software, not the salesperson, calcu-lates the most appropriate policy. You might wonder how long it will

be before the customer can simply dial into this software and dispense with the salesperson altogether.

In December an interactive shopping CD-ROM called *En Passant* was sent on trial to 30,000 people. This computer technology does more than serve up screens of photographs, prices and an 0800 number. There are over a dozen manufacturers on the disc. It gives you advice about decorating, styles, colours and ordering, and a search mechanism for finding items by key word and a way to create custom catalogues for yourself or others.

This technology trend started with home shopping catalogues. Phase two in this development is using a modem to access catalogues and databases of products on Internet (a world-wide virtual community united by computers and modem links where you can transmit pictures, sound and video imagery to any receiving computer).

Last night I wanted to buy some compact discs. I dialled an online service through the modem. I chose from a menu of possibilities and headed, on my computer screen, for a shopping area. I had access to consumer reports, news and updates on what products were on the market. It was as though I could buy virtually anything. I chose my discs, typed in my name and address and credit card details, and now await their arrival. It is a great system for those who know what they want.

The next stage from this will be a consumer perpetual motion machine already dubbed a 'vortex'. Buyers will create consumer reports and add them to libraries and databases. They will be advertising products to themselves. The database managers will just supervise the activity, deliver the product and bill the companies for their percentage. Advertising may be stood on its head. Instead of advertisers soliciting responses, they will respond to queries from potential customers.

What is on the horizon is that these services will be taken into every home via television. This move will be driven by the entertainment industry. If you can have videos dialled up onto your television screen at the push of a button, you can also market and sell any product as well. It only needs the customer to enter her credit card number on the telephone to buy. Imagine interactive advertisements built around expert computer systems that offer customised investment advice. Interactive shopping channels are already appearing. So rapid is the progress in the Electronic Bazaar that this chapter may well have become dated in the time lapse between the writing and it appearing on the bookshelves in real or virtual book shops.

The ease, reduced costs and scope of the Electronic Bazaar appear very customer friendly. But what are its drawbacks?

The GIGO principle still applies – garbage in, garbage out. You may have less choice in the Electronic Bazaar because you will be limited to what is provided online. What you do not know about, you will not miss. There will of course be ways to manipulate the system, to steer customers down particular tracks. These will be all the more effective because customers may think of computers as impersonal and objective. There is also the opposite (and more likely) possibility: too much choice – the 'Aladdin's Cave' syndrome. You are surrounded by so many good things you do not know where to start. It could well be that a special breed of salespeople emerges – Net guides. Their service will not be to sell you anything directly, but to elicit your needs and wants and then advise you where to find what you want in the maze of magic treasures behind your TV screen.

What was missing for me as I 'walked' around this Electronic Bazaar? Only the opportunity to bounce my thoughts and ideas off someone, someone with expertise from whom I could gather knowledge, someone who might be able to advise me of a more satisfying way of fulfilling my need. What I missed were the many benefits to be gained from being part of the buying/selling process with someone who would share my objective of trying to find what product was best for me.

The Electronic Bazaar is gaining momentum not solely because of the benefits that it affords, but primarily from the deficiencies of the Old Bazaar. And there is another way.

THE NEW BAZAAR

The Old Bazaar is under pressure and fading rapidly, and a new model is taking its place. The attitude summed up by the Latin phrase *Caveat emptor* (Let the buyer beware) was widespread in the Old Bazaar. Times change. Customers have become more sophisticated and litigation conscious. Television programmes have told them what to look out for and how to fight back against bad practices. Regulatory bodies have more powers to investigate and recommend changes in industrial selling practices, often backed by sanctions, and they have the will to use them. Now the Latin phrase used is *Caveat venditor* (Let the salesperson beware)!

The new model that is emerging is what we call the New Bazaar.

What are the important skills for the salesperson in this New Bazaar? Building a good relationship as a framework within which business can take place is one. To be a salesperson in the New Bazaar you must be able to view the sales/buying process from the customer's point of view as well as from your own. You need to understand what the customer is saying, both in words used and signals given, and to know that your words and signals are received as intended. And you need to believe that it is possible to sell ethically.

Also, personal congruence – when what you say and what you do reinforce each other – is essential in the New Bazaar. Congruence is the child of honesty. For a salesperson to be, and to project, this congruence, he needs to believe in his products, his company and his pricing policy, and to feel good about himself, his career path, his value and his contribution. And he needs to be managed in a way that builds his self-esteem. When a job is satisfying, there is no need to take a short-term view of selling or to use motivational training and incentive holidays as a poor substitute for a genuine desire to perform well.

Holding onto existing customers has become increasingly important in the New Bazaar. The easiest business is repeat business from satisfied customers. Measurement of success has shifted from raw figures of quantity sold to quality of business.

Manipulation is the individual counterpart of the Old Bazaar. *Influence* replaces it in the New Bazaar. They are quite different. Manipulation is the attempt to produce an outcome that the other person perceives to be at his expense either during or shortly after the interaction. It is attempting to get your own outcome at any cost to the other person. (You may or may not actually get it.) Manipulation produces a win–lose result in the short term. In the long term it is lose–lose. In sales, manipulation results in buyer's remorse, bad word of mouth about the salesperson and the company, and, in the extreme case, a bad reputation for the whole profession.

A customer who has had a bad experience is twice as likely to tell others than one who has had a good experience. Bad news travels faster and wider than good news.

Influence is universal and is the purpose of any interaction. When you communicate with another person you have an effect on him. You cannot help it. Most influence is random and purposeless, but is no less influence than premeditated influence. There is a strange idea in the culture that the moment you consciously decide you are going to influence another person it becomes manipulation, as if only random influence is good. This is nonsense. Think of all the times you seek to influence another person during the course of a day. Influence is about getting a win–win interaction in the present, and if you plan that in advance, so much the better.

NLP has many powerful influencing skills modelled from excellent communicators – including salespeople. Selling uses these influencing skills. But they are like a knife – they can be used to cut someone free or to stab him. The question is, what do you use these skills for: a win–win or a win–lose?

The results of confusing manipulation with influence may leave you either feeling bad for using your skills or bad for literally underselling yourself. Customers may mistake influence for manipulation and resist any attempt at guidance. If they have had unpleasant experiences in the Old Bazaar, you may need to hold firm to your intention to influence them and not get drawn into matching them in their Old Bazaar, thereby reverting to manipulation.

What customers want from a company is very simple: salespeople who are competent and whom they can trust, selling quality products and services.

This book aims to give some of the skills you will need for the New Bazaar. We will cover how to achieve open and honest communication with customers, how to look after your own well-being so that you can feel good about what you do, and how to manage others in a way that makes them want to treat customers in the way that customers want to be treated. Then you will be able to jump out of bed and shout, 'Hooray, another day of selling!'

PART TWO

THE SALES PROCESS

I

WHY PEOPLE BUY

Why do people buy? They buy products and services to move them from the situation they are in to a situation they would rather be in. Their 'need' is the gap between where they are now and where they want to be in the future. We, as salespeople, may believe the sales process hinges on our products. But customers do not really care about our products. They focus on their own 'need'.

It holds true that customers buy a product that will move them from their present situation to a better one whether an individual buys a bar of chocolate or a corporation places a multi-million pound order for a computer system. If your product fills that need, acts as the transportation from where they are now to where they want to be, the customers will buy it.

When you are dealing with a customer who is buying on behalf of an organisation, you will be dealing with both the customer's personal need and the organisational or company need. For example, a departmental manager may want to buy a computer system from you because he keeps losing valuable records and has to take time and trouble to find them. The organisational need may be to increase the efficiency of their after sales service. The two needs overlap but are not the same.

You cannot create a need in a customer. You may point out aspects of his situation that he may not have considered and increase his awareness of the implications, but in the end the customer decides what he needs. The sales function is to help define the limitations of the current situation, describe the desired future situation, reflect on the benefits to be derived from the move and to present your product as the way of making the move, thus creating a 'win–win' sale.

There are two sides to a need: a move towards a desired solution, and a move away from a problem situation. When there is a difference between what you have and what you want, the energy for the change may come either from dissatisfaction with the present or the attraction of a more satisfying future. Usually it is a mixture of both. Life assurance holds the double benefit of taking you towards a lump sum payout on retirement while ensuring your family avoids hardship in the event of your death. A new car can take you towards improved status and prestige and away from the fears of breakdowns, increased repair costs and the discomfort of public transport. The bigger the current problem, the stronger the motive to move. The more uncomfortable the present situation, the stronger the motivation to change. How attractive a loaf of bread appears depends on how hungry you are...

TYPES OF NEED

The first type of need is when the customer is aware and clear about the gap between her current situation and her desired situation and what she wants to buy to bridge this gap.

An obvious example of this is the retail grocery trade. Customers know they are without food, will need some in the future and go and buy some. A retailer's influence here is little more than ensuring good service to encourage the customers' return.

To fulfil this first type of need, a salesperson needs minimal selling skills, and rapport with the customer is not important. Besides, the Electronic Bazaar has virtually taken over selling to this type of need.

The second type of need is when the customer has a sense that something must change and is unclear about the product to bring about the change.

This is the domain of the skilled salesperson. He can influence the process by acting as a sounding board to clarify both present and desired states, evaluating the implications of moving from one to the other and the cost of the move. He presents products in a way that allows the customer to judge their suitability to address the newly defined need. He operates in the New Bazaar.

For example, a home-owner may be aware that his home is cold and may want it to be warm. Does he buy double glazing, cavity wall insulation or extra radiators on the central heating to satisfy this need? The double glazing salesperson, the cavity wall insulator and the plumber will have different solutions.

What of an organisation wanting to increase productivity? Do they want staff training or consultancy, and if so, what type? Or do they need a new computer system? The more unclear the need the more necessary the skills of selling.

Needs and wants

You define your 'needs' on the basis of logic. You decide what you 'want' emotionally. If I have a roomful of books spread across the floor, I need a storage system. There are many ways to fulfil that need. I may want a Scandinavian interlocking book and compact disc storage rack, taking up the whole of one wall. I may want to build shelves out of planks of wood and house bricks. Wants are how the customer fills his needs filtered through his values and feelings. Values are those things that are important to the individual, such as cost and appearance. A customer's values narrow the range of products that will meet the need.

> A successful sale is when your product matches the customer's need, values and feelings.

People never buy just the product, they buy the good feelings they think it will give them. The lure of that desired situation is the good feelings of satisfaction, security or self-esteem that go with it. Insurance policies give people a feeling of security. A new car may give a feeling of success and self-worth. An expensive product gives status.

Everybody wants good feelings. We seek out feelings of happiness and we want everything we buy to contribute towards them. Advertising is the attempt to attach good feelings to products. Advertisers want you to buy sophistication, not just clothes, or a mysterious sexual attractiveness, not just a car.

Sometimes people buy products simply because of that 'feel good' factor. They may also buy your product because being with you makes them feel good too.

Features, advantages and benefits

Features. These are the characteristics of the product, what it is.
Advantages. These are what those features do.
Benefits. These are the gains that a customer will derive from

having his needs satisfied. Customers buy benefits. They are the results of solving personal and business problems. As the saying goes, 'Do not sell the mousetrap, sell the absence of mice.'

A product will not sell itself. 'Throwing' the features of the product at the customer indiscriminately, like throwing mud at a wall in the hope that *some* of it will stick, is not selling. If I want a computer for word processing and am presented with mathematical and accounting features that I will never use, I am spending money on features I will never need. This mathematical capability will remain dormant and *I have paid for it*. This 'wasted' capability will make the product seem expensive. And it will not produce benefits. If shoes were sold in triples and not pairs, that unused shoe in the wardrobe would taint my satisfaction with the two on my feet.

So features alone do not connect with customer needs. Neither do advantages. They are purely descriptive. Customers do not care what your product can do, they do care about whether it can do something *for them*. The creative and innovative part of being a salesperson is making the links between identified needs, the features of the product and the *benefits* that the customers will derive.

SKILLS FOR THE NEW BAZAAR

So now, having looked at why people buy, what skills do you need to sell to them in the New Bazaar? How can you escape from the toils of the Old Bazaar and avoid the tentacles of the Electronic Bazaar?

1. At the top of this list we put taking care of yourself. The more you value yourself, the more others will do so. Success is more than a measure of product quantity sold, it is also about the quality of life you have selling it. Looking after yourself in an environment where, despite your best efforts, you may still be perceived as an enemy is the highest priority.

2. Before you meet a customer, you need the ability to effectively organise your work, to fill your sales pipeline with prospects, customers and repeat business.

3. Being able to build rapport with the customer is critical in the New Bazaar. Remember, a real person to relate to is what is crucially

missing from the Electronic Bazaar. The better relationships you can·
build with customers, the more they will trust you and the more
likely they will be to buy from you. In a very competitive market-
place, where one product has very little advantage over a competitor when looked at objectively, the customer is likely to do business
with the person he trusts most.

4. The ability to appreciate the customer's concerns, not just from your
   own viewpoint but from his as well, is vital in the New Bazaar. It is
   a leap of the imagination from your chair to his and one of the most
   creative parts of a salesperson's work. This mental 'shift' does not
   mean that you have to agree with customers or share their values,
   simply that you demonstrate you understand and acknowledge their
   values. You remain clear about your own point of view while
   acknowledging that another viewpoint exists. When you have both
   perspectives it is easier to mentally step to one side and look in a
   detached way at what is happening in a sales meeting. Then you will
   be able to see more clearly the next move to ensure a win–win outcome.

5. Lastly, listening and questioning skills. These are two sides of the
   same coin. By listening you will gain rapport and discover the
   questions you need to ask in order to elicit the customer's needs,
   values and concerns. Questions direct attention. The quality of the
   information you get depends on the quality of the questions you ask.

WHY PEOPLE BUY

Key Points

- People buy to fulfil a need; to move from a problem state to a more
  desirable state.
- Customers' needs are modified by their values and feelings. A successful sale meets their need according to their values.
- A product has features, advantages and benefits. Customers buy
  benefits.
- Sales skills make the connection between customer needs, product
  features and benefits derived.
- Key skills in the New Bazaar are:

taking care of yourself
organising your work
gaining rapport
being able to appreciate the customer's viewpoint
listening and asking questions

2

QUESTIONS

Questions are a cornerstone of sales success. The skill of asking good questions runs as a thread throughout the whole sales process.

What do questions do? Why do we ask them? From the point of view of the salesperson, the main reasons to ask questions are:

- to build rapport, an understanding with the customer
- to uncover the customer's needs and explore her values and concerns about the sale
- to build on existing sales

Good questions make you think. Good questions get good information. Good questions clarify what the customer means and create space to consider other possibilities.

Ask questions when you know you don't know. With questions you build up as clear an idea of the customer's need as possible, in the customer's terms. Good questions lead to the shared outcome of discovering whether there is a match between the customer's need and your product.

Questions work on the GIGO principle: garbage in – garbage out. If the question is garbage, the answer will be as well.

My favourite example of GIGO in questions is when senior members of an American company became concerned about the validity of the information they were getting from customer surveys. A fair proportion of people surveyed did not answer. The company commissioned a survey to ask people the question: 'Why would you refuse to answer opinion poll questions?' Fifty-four per cent of people they approached refused to answer.

OPEN AND CLOSED QUESTIONS

The distinction between open and closed questions is probably the most widely used in sales training. However, it is a weak distinction unless you can relate it to your purpose for asking.

Closed questions are framed in such a way as to get a 'yes' or 'no' answer. 'Did you know that already?' is an example of a closed question. Closed questions usually begin with 'is' or 'isn't', 'does' or 'doesn't'.

Open questions are designed to open a subject and explore new pathways. They usually start with 'how', 'what', 'where', 'when', 'which' or 'who' and cannot be answered by a simple 'yes' or 'no'. Open questions are one way of establishing rapport at the beginning of a meeting, when you have very little information or when your questions have to be general – 'How's business generally?' or, of course, 'How are you?'

Open questions open possibilities. Closed questions focus down on information. 'How can we use both types of question to their maximum advantage?' is an open question.

Many sales trainings stress the value of open questions, but closed questions are useful too. They do not get the customer talking, but is it always a good idea to get the customer talking? Closed questions are useful for checking information – 'Do you have a training programme scheduled in the next two months?' or 'Can you make a decision today about buying this product?'

Closed questions are also useful for checking understanding – 'I gather that delivery in the next week is essential and that you will not buy unless we can guarantee this. Is that correct?' or 'I hear you say that you need this software to have a facility for passwords to protect confidentiality. Is that right?'

These are often called reflective questions because they reflect the customer's words back to him. Whenever you are uncertain, check agreement with a closed question. This is particularly important in closing the sale when you are gaining and checking commitment to buy.

DIRECT AND MANIPULATIVE QUESTIONS

We want to make a fundamental distinction based on the purpose of the question.

Direct questions are designed to arrive at the truth. They make it easy for the customer to say what he wants to say and for you to understand what he means. The core example of a direct question is, *'What do you want?'*

Manipulative questions are designed to get customers to say what you want them to say. These types of questions aim to route the customer down a predetermined path and leave her with fewer choices. A sales training for one company we know consisted of teaching a script of over 20 sequenced closed questions. This is the Old Bazaar at its most obvious. The manipulative core question would be, *'You do want this, don't you?'*

There are many possible manipulative questioning styles. Here are a few examples. At their core they all angle for an answer that the salesperson wants to hear, rather than the one the customer might say, given more freedom. We include them in this section to separate them from the direct questions that come later and to allow you to identify whether you are using them by mistake, believing them to be the way good salespeople ask questions.

Front loading or framing

This is where you preface your question with a heavily loaded statement in order to influence the answer. For example: 'Bearing in mind the massive increase in domestic break-ins in this area, what are your views on burglar alarms for domestic premises?' This is a very different question from, 'What do you think of burglar alarms as a deterrent to domestic break-ins?'

Another variation of this is the 'safety in numbers' question. For example: 'In a recent survey, it was shown that 90 per cent of people are dissatisfied with their present furniture. Do you share this view?' Weight of numbers, in general, do not tip the scales with many people.

Polarising

This is a closed question asked in a way that directs someone to either a 'yes' or a 'no' answer. It forces them to one of the two poles and then this reply is used to lever acceptance of an unstated condition. For example: 'Are you concerned about your children's future?' Of course you are, but enough to invest in private education? 'Is safety important to you?' Yes it is, but not enough to spend twice my planned budget on a Volvo.

This style of questioning also aims to create guilt or negative feelings in the person answering. So if the person does not want to invest in private education, she may be made to think that, therefore, she does not care about her children's future. In reality there is no necessary connection between the two. Private education *might* be one way of proceeding if a parent were dissatisfied with the present school arrangements.

Negative questioning

These are questions that are phrased in the negative in order to defy contradiction. For example: 'Would you not agree to this point?' or 'Is it not true that you would like...?' To disagree runs the risks of sounding foolish as the question can assume there is a universal opinion to the contrary.

Statements as questions

These are statements followed by a silence where no response is taken as agreement. For example: 'Obviously you'll be wanting to take two of these' or 'Needless to say you'll want prompt delivery next week' or 'Clearly, a million people can't be wrong.' These types of questions presuppose an answer and are expressed in a judgemental way. Parliamentary questions are the most blatant examples. They are used not to question something seriously but to make a political point, and usually begin, 'Is it not a fact that...? or 'In view of ... do you not think that...?' Any question that starts 'clearly' or 'obviously' is obviously a judgement masquerading as a question, wasn't it?

Offering the answer

This happens when the questioner wants a specific answer or has found out the information beforehand and wants to appear knowledgeable. For example: 'How many people do you employ, about 500 or so?' 'What's important to you when you buy a car, safety I expect?'

Hidden assumptions

This is when you ask a question, but in order to answer, the customer has to accept a hidden condition. A blatant example is, 'Which pen would you like to use to sign the contract, yours or mine?' when, unless you have previously agreed to sign the contract, you are presented with a false choice.

There are more subtle ones like, 'Do you fully understand why our product is the best on the market?' In order to answer 'yes' or 'no' you have to accept the assumption that the product is the best on the market. The twist in the tale is that 'fully', implying there is something I do not yet know.

ASKING KEY QUESTIONS

NLP deals with how we think and use language. We may use the same words, but what we mean by them depends on our personal experience. Poor communication or misunderstandings are often the result of the same word meaning different things to different people. You have probably had an experience when a customer has told you something and you were sure you knew just what she meant ... until you found out what she meant was not what you had understood. Part of NLP is the art of asking key questions to avoid such misunderstandings. There is a full description of this in the book *Introducing NLP* (see Bibliography), and we will use here those parts that are particularly useful in sales.

Getting information

There is a poem by the English writer Rudyard Kipling:

> I keep six honest serving men.
> They taught me all I know.
> Their names are where and why and when,
> and who and what and how.

When covering open questions earlier in this section, we added 'which' to Kipling's list of servants but deleted 'why'.

'Why' is a special case and needs special attention.

The question 'Why?'

'Why?' is the least useful question in sales. When you ask someone why she did something you will get one of two types of answer: either the sequence of events that led up to the action, or the reason for the action.

For example: 'Why did you buy from our competitor?'

The first type of answer would be: 'Because their agent telephoned me a couple of months ago and I saw him last week. He offered what I saw as a good product, so I bought.'

The second type of answer might be: 'Because they have an excellent product at a fair price.'

'Why' questions will get you justifications as answers and little useful information.

If you ask why someone holds an opinion, he will give you excellent reasons, which you can hardly refute without losing rapport. All you will have done is made life harder for yourself by eliciting a series of justifications that the customer must now defend.

'Why?' also tends to be heard as an accusation, and people will be on the defensive. Instead of 'why', ask questions based on 'how' or 'what' to get information you can work with.

For example, if a customer says 'I do not think that will be cost-effective', rather than asking 'Why not?', ask instead:

'*How* would you compare cost-effectiveness with other products?'
'*What* do you take as a measure of cost-effectiveness?'

If a customer says, 'I think the product is overpriced', ask:

'*What* price do you think would be fair?'
'*How* did you come to that conclusion?'

Kipling was not in the selling profession, so we might amend his domestic staff a little. We will promote 'why' upstairs to the Philosophy department, where it will be kept extremely busy.

Being specific

'How', 'what', 'where', 'when' and 'who' enable you to focus specifically on what the customer wants and to receive information that has not yet emerged. How you use these questions will depend on the product you are selling and the information you need.

How do you know when you don't know something you need to know?

Some salespeople build a picture of the customers' needs like a three-dimensional sculpture in their mind. If they cannot see a detail in their mental picture, they ask a specific question to fill in the blank. The answers to their questions fill in the pieces until they are clear, checking for agreement as they proceed.

For example, the customer says, 'Let me have your proposal next week.'

Questions to ask would be:

'What do I need to put in the proposal for it to be valuable?'
'How long should it be?'
'Whom should I address it to?'
'When exactly would you like it to be on your desk?'

Every company has its own standards for evaluating proposals and your proposal might be wasted unless you find out these standards in advance.

Another example: 'I want a good after sales service.'

Questions you need to ask would be:

'Can you describe what you mean by "good after sales service"?'
'How often would you expect service visits?'
'How soon after your call would you need an engineer?'

These questions are obvious, yet it is easy to fall into the trap of thinking you know what the customer means.

Clarifying what the customer means

Never assume you know what the customer means. Philosophers and linguists cannot agree on the meaning of words and it is their job to do so. Court cases consume weeks of time and hundreds of thousands of pounds deciding how to interpret legal documents – written with the express intention of being as clear as possible.

Many people believe that every word has some eternal fixed meaning that everyone knows or should know. Would that it were so, life would be much simpler! In practice, words mean exactly what each person thinks they mean. Words describe thoughts and experience and our thoughts and experiences are unique to us. While we have a broad shared understanding, it is as if we all speak slightly different languages with our own personal Thesaurus. The nearest Japanese translation of the phrase 'Out of sight, out of mind' is 'Blind idiot'.

Many salespeople assume the customer wants and likes the same things as they themselves do. It is much safer to assume the opposite. Confine mind reading to the brightly coloured circus booths where it belongs. We know, of course, you would never consider mind reading anyway. Why mind read when you can ask directly?

Clarification of meaning will lead to shared understanding and avoid those awful loops that start, 'But I thought you meant...' Here are some of the main pitfalls in mutual understanding and the questions to ask to avoid them.

Comparisons

A customer might say, 'And I want a better service than my last financial adviser provided.' The customer is making a comparison. When you hear a comparison, this should set off alarm bells and/or warning lights. 'Better', 'worse', 'faster', 'slower', 'more' and 'less' are all comparisons. Unless you ask questions to establish a deeper understanding of *how* the customer measures value, your service or product will be compared to another and you will have no idea of the basis of that comparison.

Ask, 'Can you tell me what was unsatisfactory about your last adviser, so I can be clear on how to improve on him?'

Other examples of comparisons are:

'I want more service visits than before.'
Question: 'How many did you have and how many would you like?'

'I hope this machine is faster than my last one.'
Question: 'How fast was your last one and how fast would you like this one to be?'

Remember 'good' and 'bad' are also comparisons. A comparison sets up a standard of measurement. Unless you know what standards are being used, you will be at a disadvantage. Find out what was unsatisfactory, and then find out what the customer wants instead.

Question a comparison by asking about the standard the customer is using.

Generalities

Suppose a buyer says this: 'Our competitors are becoming very aggressive. Customers are more aware and price conscious. We need to get our act together or we will go down the tubes.'

This gives you the broad sweep of how she is thinking. But exactly which competitors are becoming competitive? How are they doing this? Which customers are more aware and price conscious? How are they showing you that?

'How exactly...?'

Business is about action and doing, so be as clear as possible what the customer or manager wants you to do. Ask not only *what* they want you to do, but *how* they want you to do it. You will need to ask some 'How exactly...' questions. 'How exactly do you want delivery?' or 'How exactly shall I arrange a demonstration?'

The other aspect of this is to ask *what* exactly the customer wants. For example:

'I would like to see what this machine can do.'
'How exactly would you like to do that?'

Creating possibilities

Absolutes

Listen for absolute words like 'always', 'never' and 'everyone'. On face value, these words stop any argument, they brook no exceptions. And yet we know that there is (nearly) always an exception to 'always'. So in response to, 'I always buy from XYZ company', you might ask, 'What is it about XYZ company that you find so satisfactory?' This will get you what XYZ company are doing that is important to the customer. You too may be able to do it better once you know the customer's terms. Follow up the first question with 'Under what circumstances would you be prepared to make an exception?' or 'If we could better that, would you consider buying from us?'

'Never' is another paradoxically limiting word. For example, 'I never have time to learn a new software program.' You have many ways to respond to this. You might say in an incredulous voice, '*Never?*' By emphasising the word you may get the customer to qualify it, 'Well, hardly ever.'

Secondly, you could ask directly for an exception: 'Are you sure there was never a time when you did?' Then you can follow up with, 'In that situation when you did, what was it that allowed you to make the time?'

'Nobody does it this way any more' could be answered by, 'Do you mean no one at all?' or 'My last client wouldn't like to be called a nobody!' (use this one only if you have good rapport) or, finally, 'What would be a reason for doing it this way? Are there any advantages whatsoever?'

Absolutes limit possibilities. *Question absolutes by asking for an exception and building on that instance.* If the customer really cannot remember an exception, ask him to imagine one.

Finally, be careful yourself in using these sort of absolute words. Customers may challenge your own absolute statements, which you will then have to qualify. Do not be drawn into statements like, 'All our customers agree with you' or 'We have never been late with a delivery' unless they are true. Only use an absolute if you can justify it absolutely.

Rules

Words that point to rules are 'should', 'must' and 'have to', with their opposites, 'shouldn't' and 'mustn't'. These can be something of a minefield, so tread with care.

Client organisations have rules. 'You must telephone first for an appointment.' 'This form must be filled in triplicate.' Comply with organisational rules where possible, for little is gained by arguing. Argue only if it is important to you and the sale, and stay respectful. The more nonsensical the rule, the more a customer may need to justify it.

However, sometimes customers will set personal limits that are unnecessary. For example, 'You must get this delivery to me by next Thursday.' This may be difficult. So explore consequences. 'What would happen if it were Friday?' The consequences may not be as disastrous as imagined.

When you hear something 'should' or 'must' happen, you can question it by asking, 'What would happen if it did not?'

For example:

'You must call next Friday.'
Question: 'I will be out of the office next Friday. Could it be another day?'

When you hear something 'shouldn't' or 'must not' happen, you can ask, 'What will happen if it did?'

For example:

'You shouldn't arrange a meeting before midday.'
Question: 'What happens if I do?'

If 'should' is a mere wooden fence, then 'can't' comes over as a brick wall. It indicates a much stronger rule. 'I can't decide yet' or 'We can't give you this order now' sound final.

Again, you can ask some key questions. 'Why not?' is blunt. 'What stops you?' is more elegant. The reason may be that the customer needs authorisation from management, is procrastinating or has a mental rule along the lines of, 'Only persistent salespeople get our orders.' Questions will get you some information you can work with; hidden rules need not prevent the customer from getting what he wants when he wants it.

> When you hear 'can't', ask about possible barriers and problems: 'What stops this from happening?'

For example:

'I can't give you the order today.'
Question: 'What stops you from giving me the order today?'

'I am afraid our department can't buy any more of your product.'
Question: 'Oh, really. What's the problem?'

Following up sales questions

You can use questions to open the possibility of more sales. As well as finding new accounts, you will want to find out how much more you can do for existing customers.

One question you can use is:

'How exactly can I serve your needs in future?'

Others are:

'How else can I help you?'
'What exactly could I and my company do to earn more of your business in the field of...'

'What's missing from our product that you would like to see?'
'Is there anyone else in your organisation or outside it that has similar needs to yours and might be interested in our product?'

HOW AND HOW NOT TO ASK QUESTIONS

Now some traps to avoid. You do not want the customer to feel she is being examined by the Spanish Inquisition. So knowing when to stop asking questions is important. Kipling's servants are very useful, but how would you feel if servants kept interrupting and disturbing you, asking (in the nicest possible way, of course) whether there was anything else you wanted?

Know when you have enough information. How detailed a picture do you build of the customer's need? Do you find yourself constantly having to go back to ask questions about aspects of the sale you missed? If this is so, it indicates you need to ask more specific questions.

The opposite and equally distracting characteristic is finding yourself continuing to ask questions and not getting any new information.

Softening the questions

Continuous questioning can be seen as aggressive and may trigger defensiveness, so intersperse your questions with other more general comments and discussion. Use softeners for your questions where necessary.

There are two ways of softening the question. The first is to use voice tone. Aggressive, harsh or loud tonality generates resistance. You can use the natural tonality of a question to help you. If your voice tonality stays level to the end of a sentence, it implies a statement. If it drops at the end of a sentence, it gives the impression of a command. If it rises at the end of a sentence, it gives the effect of a question.

Try an experiment. Say: 'You can do that' in these three different ways and notice the effect.

The other aspect to this is to keep questioning tonality out of your voice when you want to make statements.

Try this experiment. Say: 'We have an excellent product' first with an even tonality, then with a rising tonality. With the rising tonality it becomes a question, almost as if you do not believe what you are

Figure 1 Voice inflections

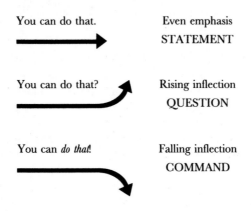

You can do that.   Even emphasis
STATEMENT

You can do that?   Rising inflection
QUESTION

You can *do that!*   Falling inflection
COMMAND

saying and you are asking the customer for reassurance. It only takes a slight shift in voice to get this effect. Some salespeople lose credibility like this through voice tone without realising what they are doing.

The second way you can soften your questions is with the form of words you use.

For example, you can precede your questions with phrases like:

'I'm interested to know whether...'
'I wonder...'
'Would you mind telling me...'

You can also 'flag' the questions. This means you warn the customer in advance so he knows that a question is coming and so may be both prepared and receptive.

For example:

'I'd like to ask a bit about...'
'I would like to clarify a point by asking...'
'If I could just pursue that point a bit further by checking...'
'Do you mind if I ask you a question about...'

Long and multiple questions

Avoid the common mistake of asking multiple questions. This is where the questioner asks a number of questions, either with the intention of creating greater clarity or of building the relationship or because he thinks he should do most of the talking.

For example: 'Was your holiday nice? I mean, was it hot? You look well, was the hotel nice? Was the food OK?'

'Yes.'

But 'yes' to which part of this machine-gun attack?

Get an answer to one question before asking another. By asking more than one at a time you will confuse the customer.

Another common mistake is the 'War and Peace' type of question. These are questions that amble on and take a walk around the forest and the fields and the beach and up a mountain and back through the forest before finally arriving. Most people find it difficult to follow a spoken question or statement of more than about 20 words.

QUESTIONS

Key Points

- Good questions are purposeful.
- Questions are used:
    to build rapport
    to uncover the customer's needs and explore her values and concerns about the sale
    to build on existing sales

- *Open questions* cannot be answered by 'yes' or 'no'. They invite ideas and discussion.
- *Closed questions* can be answered by 'yes' or 'no'. They are useful for checking information.
- *Direct questions* are about customer needs.
- *Manipulative questions* are about getting the customer to give the response the salesperson wants.

USE DIRECT QUESTIONS TO:
- Get specific information:
    use 'how', 'what', 'where', 'when', 'which' and 'who' questions
- Clarify what the customer means:
    avoid mind reading
    question comparisons
    question generalities

      question requests for action that are unclear
- Create possibilities:
        question absolutes ('never', 'always', 'no one', 'everyone')
        question rules ('must(n't)', 'should(n't)', 'have to', 'ought')
- Use questions to follow up and get more business from accounts.
- Use softeners as necessary when questioning by:
        voice tone
        phrasing
        flagging the question in advance
- Ask only one question at a time.
- Keep questions short and clear.

3

PLANNING SALES WORK

Selling is about being face to face with a customer. It is only when you are interacting with a customer that you feel you fully use your skills. Personal contact is the most exciting and creative part of the job; this is what selling *is*. Planning and organising are carried out on your own. They are not glamorous. Boring people plan. Boring people pack their suitcases days before they go on holiday. Then they arrive with every-thing they planned to take. Exciting people pack their bags moments before they are due to leave. Sometimes they have to take dirty clothes with them. And they have always forgotten something and have to use their ingenuity to get out of their predicament.

If you do not plan, it creates lots of opportunity to demonstrate your resourcefulness, reactivity skills and your dislike of conformity and convention. Yet organisation and planning underpin all other skills and create more time for the more exciting parts of the job. Also, how you plan and organise your work and time directly influences your sales figures and how much you earn. There's little point being great at face-to-face skills if you hardly ever get face to face with people because of poor organisation. Planning well ensures qualified customers and more productive meetings. Poor planning means wasted time. A survey carried out with software salespeople found 32 per cent of their time was spent *waiting*, 24 per cent on administration and meetings, 5 per cent on service calls and only 39 per cent selling.

For those of you with management aspirations, being organised is essential. In the main, the only time a salesperson is promoted into man-agement purely because he is the top performer is when he threatens to leave and the company can ill afford to lose his skills to a competitor. Normally people are promoted because they have an understanding of the sales process, know the products, market-place and company, relate well to others and will provide senior manage-ment with good results and minimum problems. One way the last criterion is judged is by looking at how well organised someone is.

Organisation is not the opposite of creativity and has little to do with tidiness. It is not about being dull. It is very simple. It is deciding what you want, what you are going to do to get it and how long it is going to take. If you neglect this, you will miss selling opportunities, waste time with poorly qualified clients and ultimately spend *more* time on becoming organised than it warrants.

This section of the book will demonstrate how you can do the minimum for the maximum results. If you are already well organised, congratulations. This section will give you some new choices and some ways you might become even more effective.

There are four main stages to good organisation:

1. Goal-setting.
2. Breaking goals into manageable tasks.
3. Setting priorities.
4. Managing your tasks through time.

GOAL-SETTING

Setting goals or objectives is at the heart of professional success. Without goals you have nothing to plan or organise. Goals are what you want to achieve. Success is the progressive realisation of your worthwhile, predetermined goals. You set goals that will take you from where you are now to where you want to be and you enjoy the journey as well as the final achievement. Journeys take time and how you use your time is important. Time management is a misleading term. You cannot manage time. Time manages itself. You can only manage what you do in the time there is. And everyone has the same amount – 24 hours a day. Manage your goals and time will manage itself.

As you work through the following goal-setting process, it is essential that you write down your results.

You do not need to use your brain as a filing cabinet. It is the wrong shape and made of the wrong material. As Sean Connery said as Indiana Jones' father in 'The Last Crusade', when asked to remember some information he had scribbled onto a piece of paper, 'I wrote it down so I wouldn't *have* to remember it.'

- Think of your most important sales projects at the moment. They may be short, medium or long-term projects. What are your goals

for these projects? What do you want to achieve from each? Summarise it in a sentence.
- Give each project a deadline.
- Go through each project in turn, checking and writing down the following points:

> Think in the positive: towards what you want to achieve, not what you want to avoid. 'I want to make a sale to company X at the sales presentation on Wednesday' is positive. 'I do not want any problems with company Y account' is negative. You cannot achieve a negative. Put down what you want, not what you don't want.

> Make sure you can measure your success. How will you know you have achieved that goal? What will you see, hear or feel when you have achieved that goal? If your goal is to sell to company X, then you will want to see their order, hear confirmation and feel elated by your success.

> Check the resources you have that will help you achieve the goal. What people can help you? What contacts, personal qualities, tools and skills do you have that will help you?

> Now think in more detail. Who exactly will be involved? Where will it happen? When will it happen? How long will it take?

> Explore the consequences for yourself and other people. Will other people have to help you and can you count on that? Will it mean you have to work 20 hours a day for the next week? What will you have to give up to achieve these goals?

> Finally is it realistic in view of what you have discovered so far?

Check each of your goals through the SMART format. Is it:

Specific
Measurable
Achievable
Realistic
Timed

BREAKING GOALS INTO MANAGEABLE TASKS

Now look at the goals and ask yourself what has to happen for you to achieve these? What prevents you from having them right now? You can do this in two ways.

1. Look forward from now to when you will complete the task. What are the steps you will have to take to achieve that goal?
2. Imagine you have already achieved the goal. Now imagine looking back to the present. What are the steps and stages you see leading from then to now?

Break each goal into no more than seven tasks that you need to do to achieve your main goals.

Make an action plan of the tasks you will do in a rough sequence.

Figure 2

The goal: To establish XYZ company as a customer.

Evidence: I would see the order sheet, hear verbal confirmation over the telephone, my manager would praise me and I would feel excited by the achievement.

Resources: My own sales skills, the technical expertise in the service department, my manager's support and encouragement and the interest and possible involvement of the managing director.

Who, where, when: I would be involved with my manager and managing director. For XYZ, there would be involvement from their head of purchasing, the end user and Financial Director. The sales discussions would take place at XYZ's office with a demonstration being conducted in our showroom. The process will take three weeks to instigate and six months to conclude.

Implications: The positive implications are that I will gain financially, my prestige and profile will be raised, and the way in which I handle this account might identify me as management material. The possible negative implications are that I will have to put in a great deal of effort now for reward later. This might

---

reduce my short- to medium-term results and I will have to work longer hours. (Both of these need to be handled within my plan.)

What will I have to give up? To achieve this goal I will have to cut back on social activity. This will impact on my partner. (In order for this issue not to sabotage the achievement of my goal I will need to have, as part of my plan, a discussion with, and support from, my partner.)

Realistic? The goal is realistic. XYZ currently use products similar to ours. We have a competitive advantage over the current supplier on quality and delivery times. XYZ have considered using us in the past and failed to because of the way we handled the sales discussions.

Manageable tasks:
– Discuss with my partner the implications of the short-term increased work load.
– Agree the best initial approach to XYZ with my manager.
– Gain an understanding that short-term results may drop.
– Check that resources are available.
– Make phone calls to establish a contact name.
– Talk to other people who have sold to XYZ.
– Talk to those involved in our failed attempt to sell to XYZ in the past.

Computer software is available that will take you through the whole goal-setting process and print out the results for you (see Business Consultancy section).

This process divides your outcomes into a series of small achievable tasks that need to be done on a daily basis and will thoroughly prepare you for sales reviews with your manager. It will also help you to avoid the two big traps of time management and goal-setting:

1. One trap is getting lost in the minutiae of small daily tasks and losing sight of the goal they are designed to achieve. A telephone call in itself is a small thing and is not likely to fire you with enthusiasm, but when you think of it as a step towards that big sale you have planned, it is easier to make.
   Connect your small routine tasks to your goals.

2. The second trap is being overwhelmed by the size of a task, biting off more than you can chew and thinking you have to do it all at once. Our brains have a habit of presenting us with our goals all at once. How do you eat an elephant? One bite at a time. You can only do one step at a time and you only have to do one step at a time. Any time a task seems too much to contemplate, break it down into smaller tasks.
Break large goals into manageable tasks.

SETTING PRIORITIES

Now you have your list of tasks and can begin to think on a day-to-day basis.

Divide your tasks into two categories:

Urgent   **Not Urgent**

Urgent activities are those you have to do. They may be directly or indirectly connected to your goals. Urgent activities demand your immediate attention. Not urgent tasks are easy to categorise. They are everything else.

Next, divide all the tasks into two further categories:

Important   **Not Important**

Important activities get results and are directly connected to your goals. They are what you value about your work. Stephen Covey has an excellent section on time management using these distinctions in his book *The Seven Habits of Highly Effective People*.

• The *urgent and important* activities you have to deal with, make them a priority. If most of your time is spent in this area then you may be the sort of person that generates emergencies too easily. If a lot of your time seems to be taken up here, notice how you may be contributing to the situation by neglecting the work that is important but not urgent. When you leave important but not urgent tasks long enough they will become urgent. Spending time fire fighting and dealing with emergencies is stressful and unnecessary.

A lot of tasks in the urgent and important category also make planning difficult. They are time consuming and distracting and, dare we say it, exciting? After a day full of urgent and important work you really feel as if you are earning your money. But these urgent tasks often do not get you closer to your goals, only stave off a disaster. As you plan better, you will find that less of your time is taken up with them. One way of knowing you are better organised is noticing that you spend less time on these frantic tasks. You do not have to work harder, just *smarter* – a distinction not appreciated by workaholics. Workaholics are addicted to work, not to results, or success.

• The *important and not urgent* activities are where you will get the best results with the least effort. They are what get you your goals. As you manage your time and projects more effectively you will find more of your activity falling into this area. This is where you can take action to stop many of the crises that take up your time. There will always be crises, but you can keep them to a minimum. Goal-setting, building good relationships with clients, long-term planning and preparing for meetings also come into this area.

• The *urgent but not important* are likely to be the biggest time wasters because we often think they are important. These are usually very short-term activities and nearly always involve other people expecting you to do things. There are two main culprits:

> The telephone – it does not just ring, it insists, like someone tugging at your sleeve incessantly. It has a power over us because it won't tell us who is on the other end unless we pick it up. Could it be that important client we have been waiting for? That vital address? An emergency?
>
> Be honest, probably not. If you are expecting an important call, then all that is needed is that someone answers the telephone. If you have an assistant, he may be able to handle the call, refer it to someone else or take the message for you to ring back at *your* convenience.
>
> If you do not have an assistant, work out a deal with your colleagues so the telephone is always covered by someone. Use a voice mail system or take the telephone off the hook.
>
> Mail comes in three categories: the junk you can throw away; the letters that need only a glance and need no response apart from filing; and those that need some response. Divide this last group into urgent/not urgent and important/not important and work them into your day.

• Finally the *not urgent and the not important* (and also not necessary) activities. You probably know what these are already. Remember the saying,

'Killing time is not murder, it's suicide.' The not urgent and not important activities need our co-operation before they become a problem.

Some travel time can fall into this category. Face-to-face meetings are expensive for sales companies and business customers. More business can and is being done by telephone.

Separate these activities that achieve no results from activities like relaxing and looking after yourself, however. Your health is certainly important and could be urgent.

Taking on too much

Lots and lots of little raindrops can add up to a storm, so pace yourself. Taking on a lot to please others will have the opposite effect if you let things slide due to work pressure. The words 'no' and 'later' are wonderfully satisfying to say. You may dress them up or you may be blunt, depending on who you are talking to. It could be hard to say 'no' to a manager. Try something like this.

'Sure I'll do it, just let me tell you about what I'm working on at the moment.'

Show her the projects you have. The more carefully they are organised, the more impressive they will be.

Then say something like, 'So I've calculated that these will fill my time pretty much for the next few days. Doing what you have just asked me is going to disturb one of these. Which one would you like me to cancel or reschedule so I can do this latest task?'

What we have said so far is important and not new. We all realise how important good time management is, and one way to really bring this home is to review last week and calculate how much of your time was spent on client contact. Now work out the value of this time by apportioning the revenue you produced per hour of face-to-face time. It could be thousands of pounds. By creating just one more hour of face-to-face contact you could increase your results by thousands of pounds with no improvement in your sales ability.

So, what could stop you from using your time to get the results you want?

MANAGING YOUR GOALS THROUGH TIME

This is the area where NLP can make a unique contribution.

Time-management schemes seem to be common sense, yet many people do not and cannot use them. They are based on an assumption that we all experience time in the same way. We do not. The irony is that time management appeals to people who are *already* organised and think that way. It comes naturally to some people and not to others, and this is because of the different ways we experience time *subjectively*. *That* is the realm of NLP.

If you find managing your work difficult, understanding how you experience time will make a tremendous difference. If you find it easy, it will make it easier still.

Think about how you experience time in your mind. We measure time externally in terms of distance and motion – a moving hand on a clock face – but we all have unique ways of sorting our memories and planning for the future. Do the following short experiment and find out how you experience time.

Time lines

Most people experience time as a line connecting past and future. Think for a moment about something that happened yesterday. Something you saw and heard. Now think about an experience that occurred a few weeks ago. Both are in the past. From which direction do these experiences seem to come from? From the right or left, up or down, in front or behind you?

Now take an event you anticipate happening in the future. From which direction does that seem to come from?

When you get a sense of where the past memories and the future hopes come from, notice how they are connected by a line. This is your time line. Notice where 'now' appears on the time line. Does it seem to be within your body or outside it?

Time lines fall into two broad categories. The first type is where you experience 'now' as being outside your body, usually just in front of you. It is as if you can be a little outside the stream of time, watching it passing. Usually both your past and future experiences seem to be in front of you on a line running from right to left. This is called *through time*.

The second type is where you experience 'now' as being inside your body. This is called *in time*. If you are an in time person, very often your time line will have the past behind you and the future in front of you.

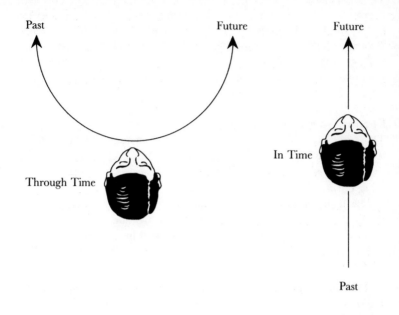

Figure 3 In time and through time line

There has been much research on time lines in NLP and you may like to read some books that deal with them in more detail (see Bibliography: *Time Line Therapy and the Basis of Personality* by Tad James). Planning is much easier for people with a through time line. As time is laid out in front of them, it is easier to see and plan the sequence of tasks. They will also expect to make and keep appointments precisely. They find it easy to establish deadlines and take them seriously, while expecting others to do the same. Through time is the time line that is prevalent in the business world, where 'time is money'.

A person with an in time line is much more focused in the present moment, experiencing things as they happen. He can literally 'put the past behind him'. He will tend to live in a less ordered way and typically will not set deadlines. In time people may seem less dependable and interpret appointments more flexibly. They do not lack the energy or skill, they just do not necessarily connect what they are involved in right now with a planned future.

There is nothing inherently superior about either through time or in time. It all depends what you want to do. There are many activities where you will want to be fully in the moment. That is when you want to be in time. Many salespeople are mostly in time, as it gives them their focus on the customer in sales meetings. For planning, goal-setting and business meetings a through time line is better.

There are no prizes for guessing which type of person makes up time-management schemes and finds them easy to use! Through timers preach the time-management gospel.

Choosing your time line

You can change your time line for certain activities, although do not try to change it generally.

Use a through time line for deciding your goals, dividing them into tasks and setting priorities.

The first step is checking that you are through time when you do this and changing to through time if you are not. (When you have finished, you can change back to your normal in time line.)

This is the process:

1. Working in a quiet place, imagine stepping off your time line as though you were stepping onto a pavement in order to look back at a road. Now imagine that you can see the road stretching out in both directions. Now make one end of the road represent the future and the other end the past. You will be standing by the part of the road that represents the present.

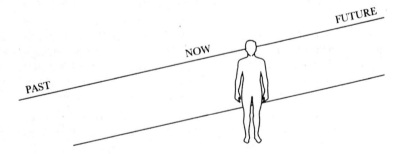

Figure 4 Stepping off your time line

2. Now go through the goal-setting process as described before. Divide the goals into smaller tasks and set priorities. Mentally map all your tasks from your written plan onto this road, your time line, as you

imagine it in front of you. Lay out the tasks on this road so that the further away they are, the further in the future you will do them. Immediate tasks will be the closest. (If imagining this process does not work for you, you can carry it out on the floor by writing each task on a piece of paper and arranging them in sequence in front of you.)

3. As you divide the goals into tasks and you set deadlines for their completion, imagine yourself carrying out each task in the future. Imagine each task successfully accomplished. Imagine the satisfaction you will feel as each task successfully slots into place.

4. Now mentally rehearse what you want to happen. Imagine your working day. Identify what naturally occurring breaks will remind you to look at your plan. Imagine yourself looking at the plan during these. Or you might imagine yourself asking a well organised, through time friend or colleague to remind you.

5. When you have finished, change the time line back to your normal one by stepping back into the present moment and restore your normal time line.

(Although you can carry out this process from this book, for some people it may prove difficult. It is easier to work with a group or as part of a sales training course.)

Now you have your goals, tasks and deadlines mapped on your written plan and your mental time line. If you are a through time person you may find you already do this naturally without even being aware of it.

Keep your written plan with you at work. Look at it during naturally occurring breaks in the day. Whenever you look at your plan imagine it in your time line. Some tasks you will see in your past time line as completed. Others are still in your future time line. Every occasion you do this will strengthen the association between the written plan and being through time. Building associations like this is called *anchoring* in NLP. We associate objects and events to feelings and actions. By repeatedly linking your written list with your action plan through time, you build a strong association. And it is a pleasant association because you have already imagined accomplishing the tasks and anticipated the good feelings of success.

This process makes planning and organisation much easier and more effective and less stressful. It can also be used to prepare a good emotional state (see pp.157–9). Here, you have made sure that the through time is anchored to the sight of the work plan. You keep your focus as an in time person for other things where it works well for you.

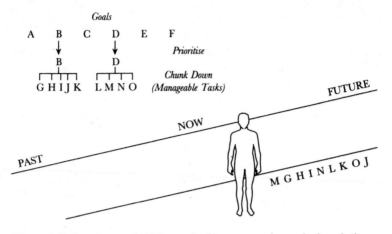

Figure 5 Goal-setting – prioritising – chunking – managing goals through time

MANAGING YOUR TERRITORY

How you manage your territory will be greatly influenced by the following factors:

How you are measured: If management prefer their salespeople to burn lots of petrol and have backache as a demonstration of commitment then you are likely to organise your territory in a way that provides both pieces of evidence for them.

Where you live: If you have a long journey to arrive on patch, you will plan your territory differently than if you lived in the middle of it.

How frequently you need to see customers/call rate: Some sales jobs require 15 calls a day, others three a week. Obviously this divergence will impact on how territories are planned.

Your attitude towards your work: As with other forms of organisation, territory planning is probably a better indication of motivation and attitude than is performance in front of a customer.

Your favourite radio programmes: We may, knowingly or unknowingly, plan our territories and journeys to ensure that we can listen to our favourite programmes while travelling.

How reactive you need *to be:* If problems do arise that you will need to resolve, you will need to build in access to all parts of your territory.

The business balance: In some territories small areas may produce high percentages of business. Business density should influence your plan more than physical acreage.

The overall size: The city of London will provide different criteria than Milton Keynes.

When planning your territory it may be useful to plan it as you would a sight-seeing holiday. For it is at these times that we tend to organise ourselves in a way that allows us to see the most with the minimum travelling costs. The 'mean tourist' hat will enable you to see your territory not as somewhere you need to be for 40 hours a week, but as land from which you need to glean the most with the minimum of cost and effort. It can reduce the temptation to return to the office (the holiday hotel) after each call.

There are various ways of dividing up a territory. The 'pizza' plan, where you allocate a day to each of the sections of a pizza, is in common use. The 'squared matrix' is similar but based on superimposing graph lines over the territory.

The key to effective territory planning is to use a method that has clear, business objectives and rationale – and any plan is better than the 'I'll go where I fancy' approach.

ORGANISATION AND PLANNING

Key Points

- Good planning means you spend less time planning and more time selling.
- Goal-setting is the first step to good organisation:
  pick your important sales goals at the moment
  use the SMART check – Specific, Measurable, Achievable, Realistic, Timed
- Break the goals down into achievable tasks:
  write down the tasks
  prioritise the tasks
- Divide the tasks into *Urgent* and *Not Urgent.*
- Divide them into *Important* and *Not Important.*
- Concentrate your efforts on the *Not Urgent and Important* activities.

TIME
- There are two ways to experience time:
  In time is experiencing the present moment as inside your body. Your time line usually has your past behind you, your future in front of you.
  Through time is experiencing the present moment as outside your body. Time passes externally. Your time line usually has both past and future in front of you.
- Do planning and goal-setting with a through time line.
- Set up an automatic association between looking at your written plan and having a through time line.

TERRITORY
- Wear your 'mean tourist' hat.

PROSPECTING
AND INITIAL CONTACT

4

Remember a time when you were really convinced and congruent that your product met the customer's need. In spite of your conviction, you may or may not have been successful. The customer may have been convinced or your best efforts may have gone to waste. To understand why the customer may not have been convinced, despite your commitment, remember now when you were the unconvinced customer of another salesperson. His arguments obviously made sense to *him*, but you just didn't see how they applied to you.

Now, has there ever been a time when you've watched the selling/buying process taking place between two other people and you've known that you understood what was happening between them better than either of them did? That position is very useful sometimes, particularly when the salesperson and the customer are not connecting.

Being in your own reality, knowing your own point of view, is called being in *first position* in NLP. Good salespeople have to have a strong first position to sell the product congruently.

Being aware of the reality and point of view of another person, in this case your customer, is called being in *second position* in NLP. You will have experienced it when you feel in accord with another person, almost as if you know what she is thinking. Without a second position, you cannot influence the other person because you do not know how the world seems to her.

To be in a position where you can appreciate both points of view is called being in *third position* in NLP.

The more you can appreciate both the customer's position and the whole sales process, the more selling success you will have. In our sales trainings we have people role play as themselves in order to focus on their own goals and skills (first position), and role play the customers so that they can develop a better understanding of what customers look for and respond to (second position), and we have them review both sides of the process by watching it on video, so that they can be objective and detached (third position).

As salespeople it is all too easy to become entrenched in first position, to strive for your own gain with no regard for the customer (no second position), and no ability to stand back objectively to view what is taking place between you and the customer (no third position). It helps our understanding of the sales process to view it from all three positions before we focus on our particular responsibilities.

The Sales Process

Stages	Salesperson's viewpoint	Customer's viewpoint
Qualifying	Prospecting	Recognising needs
Meeting	Establishing rapport	Initial impressions
	Eliciting needs and values	Reviewing choices
The sale	Dealing with objections and concerns	Resolving problems
	Closing	Deciding
Customer service	Implementation Follow up/referrals	Using

PROSPECTING

The first step in this chain is prospecting for customers. Prospecting means looking for a precious resource. An oil company does not drill hundreds of holes in the pious hope that one will strike lucky. They survey and gather a lot of information before deciding where they will drill. Drilling an oil well is an expensive business.

In sales, prospecting includes identifying and qualifying your customers – establishing who they are and that they have a need and an initial interest in what you can supply. The golden rule is: *Don't waste your time with people who have no need for your product.*

A sales call is expensive. Each year McGraw-Hill publishes figures on the cost of a sales call. The 1988 figures show the cost in the United States was $260 and in Britain $303.82. If you make three to six calls to make a sale, the cost of selling becomes frighteningly high.

Picture your current pipeline of customers. Part of your overall organisation and planning is to make sure you have a constant flow of customers going through every stage of this process, that there are no 'bottlenecks'. To do this you need to be operating through time. You have to address the whole cycle for any one part of it to work well. If an oil company invests most of its money in refineries, it will look foolish when its flow of crude oil dries up and there is no funding to prospect for more wells. The refineries will have nothing to refine. Likewise, if you spend a great deal of time closing, you may run out of customers to close.

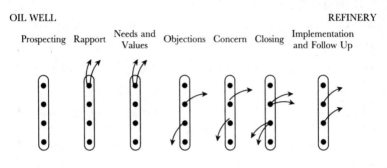

Figure 6 Pipeline

To ensure this does not happen, work out your rate of closed sales to prospects. If you close 10 per cent of your sales, you need 10 times that number of prospects in the pipeline all the time.

Building a customer pipeline

How do you build your pipeline? Marketing strategies and advertising will put you in contact with possible customers. Your company may buy lists of customers and then direct mail them, or you may be involved in cold calling.

- Think of the benefits of your product.
  What problems does it solve?
  How could you design some questions that would discover whether a prospective customer had that problem?

- When prospecting companies, look to industries that are ready to grow or actively growing, rather than those that are declining or stable. While it is hard to predict the future, the high technology and communication industries are the obvious candidates in the mid nineties.

- You can specialise in part of the total market.

  Which part are you attracted to?

  Which type of customers do you find easy to deal with?

  Which section do you best understand?

  By specialising you become more aware of the needs of that particular market segment. As you become better known and gain in expertise, the corporate grapevine will feed you customers. You do not have to sell to every sector.

Using your customer base

Draw up the profile of your typical customers. What do they have in common?

If you sell to organisations, draw up a profile of the type of company where you have been successful: the industry, size and company culture. Now draw up a profile of the individual buyer within the company. Which level of management are they in? Which department?

Look again at your customer base. Who are your worst customers? Who do you wish you had never sold to? Develop a 'problem profile' so you can avoid difficult customers in future.

Satisfied customers are your best resource in prospecting. They will recommend your product to other people. Dissatisfied customers will put others off. Satisfied customers give repeat orders and referrals.

Referrals

Referrals are qualified contact names given to you by a person who is in good standing with the referral name. How do you get referrals? By asking. Why should someone give you a referral? Because satisfied people like to share. Others following their decisions adds credibility to their decisions.

'Who do you know who would be interested in this product?' is too general a way to ask for a referral. Customers will be reluctant to mentally sort through all their contacts.

'Mr Jones, we find that organisational development managers of medium-sized companies like your own are particularly interested in our product. *Who* do you know in this area that I could contact?' is an approach that gives a tighter focus and helps your customer with his sorting.

CONTACT LEVEL

Contact level is influenced greatly by the type of products you are selling, whether or not the client company is using a competitor's product and whether your type of product is new or innovative. It is also influenced by cost. The more expensive your product or service, the higher up into management you will have to go to authorise purchase.

Here are some of the different approaches you may consider.

Top down

This means going to the top first, as high as you possibly can, at least board level, but preferably to the managing director. The benefits to the salesperson of this point of contact are that if you can sell the top person on your idea or concept and then have to deal with decision influencers or users of the product later, you do so with the authority of a senior manager. People will deal with you as though you were a representative of senior management and not an outsider trying to get in. Also, a senior manager is more likely to have an umbrella view of the company as opposed to a departmental or parochial view. This creates greater opportunity to find areas of need.

The drawback to this approach is that senior people, in the main, are very difficult to contact. They book appointments with reluctance and a long time into the future. There is very little you can do about this, except be persistent. Also, they tend to be mean with time so when you do make your presentation, keep it short and simple, give them the big picture.

If top down works for your products and market-place, then use it. Of all the approaches, it has the fewest pitfalls. If you are wasting your time, at least you find out early.

Middle up

Middle up means having initial contact at departmental head level with a view to establishing an 'internal salesperson' or 'sales guide'. This is someone who is committed to the benefits of your product. He will give you invaluable advice on who to see and how to approach meetings.

The benefits of this approach are that you enlist the services of someone seen to have no personal axe to grind, not biased by financial reward, who knows the internal workings and politics of the client company and will work on your behalf when you are not there.

The drawback to this approach is that the buying criteria of the internal salesperson may be different from that of the decision-maker. The internal salesperson may have a limited awareness of corporate aims, goals and policies. Competitive products may be under consideration by the actual decision-makers. Also, if the internal salesperson leaves the client company, then interest in your products may go with him.

Bottom up

This is where initial contact is made at a fairly low level, usually with the end user of the product. If the cost of the product is low enough to be bought within end user budgets, there is no need to sell a broader concept to the company. This approach works by having others observe the use of your product and being 'sold' by the benefits derived.

This approach is not as weak as it may seem. Many corporate personal computer policies have been shaped in this fashion. Where a large manufacturer main frame policy exists it is unrealistic and time consuming to try to shift the policy in one go. Far better to chip away at the monolith slither by slither until it is gone.

Whichever approach you use, you need eventually to talk to the person or people in the company who:

- Know the organisational needs in the area of your product or service, or deal with the problems your product addresses.
- Have the money available and the decision-making power to authorise purchase, or who will be influential in doing so. When you enter an account, find out the defined purchasing channel for your product.

If your initial contact is at a high level there are also two other people you may need to see and influence. There is the person who is responsible for using the product or for persuading others to use it. Also, there is often a person who will evaluate the technical aspects of the product.

A team of salespeople from a computer hardware company were selling a large computer system into an organisation. They spent time with the company technical experts, explaining the system. The main buying criteria for these experts was whether the system used the newest technology. They knew that if it did not, it would be redundant very soon and would not interface with the rest of the company systems. The technical experts recommended the system highly and the decision-maker signed the order. However, the users were not properly consulted. They were unhappy on two counts. First, they felt the new system was imposed on them. Secondly, and more important, the system was not easy to use for the work they had to do. Their criteria were not about the technology, but about how it did the tasks they were responsible for. The users complained, resisted using the system and the results were disappointing.

PROSPECTING AND INITIAL CONTACT

Key Points

* The sales process will appear differently to customer and salesperson.

PROSPECTING
* Good prospecting strongly influences sales success.
* Do not waste your time with people who have no need for your product.
* Build up your prospect list so your sales pipeline is always full.
* Build up a customer profile so you can qualify prospects.
* Get referrals from satisfied customers.

CONTACT LEVEL
* There are three main initial approaches:
    Top down
    Middle up
    Bottom up
* Where possible, sell to contacts who:
    are aware of the organisational needs
    have the decision-making power to purchase
* Consult the technical experts in the organisation.
* Consult the users.

5

THE TELEPHONE

Most prospecting and initial sales contact is on the telephone. So how do you make the best use of it? On the telephone, all you have is your voice and the words you speak to make a good first impression and put across what a trustworthy and professional person you are. Many salespeople find this absence of visual communication a drawback. Not being able to see the customer's body language, facial expressions and gestures is considered limiting. However, the telephone can make initial contact easier and more effective. How come? Because you can concentrate on and become a master of that one sensory channel without being distracted by the others.

Gaining rapport with your voice

Gaining rapport, oneness, with a person is gaining their trust, establishing a relationship where each is responsive to the other. It is listening to and appreciating the other person's viewpoint. But how will she know what you are really like over the telephone? How can you show that you are responsive and willing to be influenced by what she says?

You have two ways: what you say and the way you say it. The singer and the song. We alter our voice qualities automatically when we want to influence and form a positive relationship with a person on the other end of the telephone. Research in the late 1960s that has been confirmed repeatedly by further studies shows that the impact of a communication is determined by body language, voice tone and words. The voice tone is over five times more influential than words to convey a trustworthy message. Think back to a recent telephone conversation. You probably remember the person's voice and the general tenor of the conversation more than the exact words she used.

So in order to gain rapport with the customer, you 'voice match' her – you listen to what she says and use some of her key words and phrases when you respond. And, as well as her words, you match aspects of her voice, such as speed of speech, volume and pitch.

Imagine two musicians improvising a duet. The more they establish common rhythm and harmony, the more satisfying the piece will sound. To achieve this, each listens to the other to blend his sound to create the music. However, be careful. Matching voice tone does not mean imitating, but harmonising.

Start by matching volume and speed, because as well as being important, they are the simplest qualities to match. A person talks at much the same speed they are comfortable listening to. As you become more practised and comfortable doing this, you can match other voice qualities, such as pauses, timbre and rhythm. However carefully you prepare your script and however well you know the technical details, if your voice puts the customer off, he will not respond. But when you voice match, your voice *cannot* put the customer off because it's like his own.

Studies of top telephone salespeople confirm that they voice match. The most successful have a voice for every occasion. Their voice shifts automatically to suit the person they are talking to. It is likely you, also, voice match already, although you may not be aware of it. People voice match naturally from the very first words they speak, because something inside, this desire to relate to others, tells them to.

There are four additional skills you can use to establish rapport on the telephone:

- Make a mental picture of the customer. It does not matter how accurate this is, what it does is give a sense of a real person behind the disembodied voice. When you do this, you will hear interest, amusement, boredom, irritation or delight expressed through the voice and actually see these on the person's face in your mind's eye.

- Clear your mind of self talk or internal dialogue. (Internal monologue is a more accurate description.) To voice match, appreciate and respond to the customer, you have to listen to him and not to yourself.

- Match the customer's own words or phrases when you ask questions and check back that you understand. The reason he uses those precise words is that they convey what he means. By using them in turn, you not only let him know that you are listening to what he says, but also that you respect their meaning, rather than paraphrasing and distorting it.

- Use the skills in the self-management section of this book to ensure you are in a good state, a good frame of mind. When you have a lot of calls to make with a similar message, it can be tedious. The customer you call may hear tedium in your voice and take it personally. Prepare well. When you feel good about what you say, what you say sounds good.

Be clear about the purpose of your call

What is the *minimum* you want to achieve from this call? What is your purpose in calling? It may be to arrange a face-to-face meeting. You may be checking with a customer that all is well. There may be a problem and you want to gather information, rather than suggest a solution. Occasionally you may want to close a sale. And you do not have to limit yourself to one goal. In fact, whatever else you want to achieve, set a goal to build relationship with every call. But do not let your goal blind you to other opportunities that come up naturally.

INITIAL CONTACT

When you talk to a prospective customer, match her initial greeting exactly. If she says 'Good morning', say the same back. Match the voice for volume and speed.

Check that you are speaking to the right person. If you have a name from a direct referral or a chain, ask whether you are speaking to her: 'Is that Susan Black?'

If you do not have a name, say something like, 'I want to speak to the person in the training department who deals with software training. Are you that person?' Ask very specifically.

Give your name and your company. Then ask for her name if you do not already have it.

If your first call is to a referral, ask whether the original customer has contacted the person. Say something like, 'Good morning. I am John Jones from XYZ. I am a software consultant. [Pause here slightly for the customer to take that in.] I recently was able to help Frank X of Y Corporation. He gave me your name and said you might be interested in talking to me. Has Frank told you about me yet?'

Pause again, and let your customer search their memory. The 'yet' is a quick way of saying that Frank said he would.

Next ask, 'Is this a convenient time to speak for a few minutes?' If the person says, 'No', arrange a more convenient time to call back.

Say, 'I appreciate you are busy. When can I call back so we can talk for a few minutes?' Agree a definite time and then thank them for their time, say 'Goodbye' and hang up. Call back when you said you would.

DURING THE CONVERSATION

Chaining

This approach works well if you are selling into middle management, or when you have a more multifaceted product or service that might be used in different ways by different departments. For example, if your company sells communication skills training, you may not be sure of the best person to speak to. It could be the personnel, training or human resources department.

If you do not have a referral, pick a job title and department that you think may be able to help you. You may decide to start by contacting the training department. Telephone and ask to speak to the training manager. Ask for her name. When you get through, say something like:

'Hello, is that Jane Smith? My name is John Jones from XYZ. Perhaps you have heard of us?'

Follow this with, 'I'm looking for the person who deals with communication skills training resources. Are you that person?'

If she says 'Yes', then continue by explaining who you are and what you sell.

If she says 'No', then explain a little about your product until she says, 'I think you need to speak to Marsha Davenport in IT.'

The conversation will be easy, because you are not selling to her directly.

Thank the training manager and then either write a letter to Marsha Davenport in IT or call her. In each case you can say that Jane Smith, the training manager, suggested her name.

When you do speak to Marsha Davenport, she may indeed be the right person to talk to or she may refer you on in turn. She may also give you leads and referrals into other companies. Some chains lead to good sales, others peter out. You need only make one cold call: the first one – and that one is easy because it is not really a sales call, it is initially a request for help.

If your first contact does not seem to understand what you are selling, this is a sure sign that you are on the wrong level. You need to be higher. Call again to a higher management level.

At any stage a contact may be rude or hang up. This is nothing to do with you. He may be having a bad day or had some negative experiences with your competitors. He does not even know you, or your product, and now he probably never will. When this happens, write his number on a piece of paper and guess some reason he acted the way he did. (Make it as outrageous as you like – he lost his cufflinks down the sink, spilt coffee down his suit, his train was delayed and he was late for work.) Transfer any bad feelings you may have about the call onto the piece of paper, either by writing them down or drawing something to represent them. Now breathe out, crumple the paper and throw it with as much force as you wish into the wastepaper basket.

Guiding the conversation

Whoever is asking questions is directing and guiding the conversation. During the call, use questions to gather information and define the customer's position. Keep track of your level of rapport all the time; continue to match the speed and volume of the customer's voice.

Telephone conversations have unwritten rules about taking turns to speak in order to avoid a free-for-all. After you ask your question, pause and allow the other person to take his turn and answer. Also, do not ask more than one question at a time and do not attempt to say too much in one turn.

Use different perspectives

Remember the three ways to track a conversation:

- *Your own point of view.* Why am I calling? What am I selling? What do I want to say?
- *The customer's point of view.* What is she feeling? What does she want? Why is she talking to me?
- *The detached point of view.* How is this conversation going? Are we in rapport? What is the most useful question to ask next?

Being able to keep track of these three views is a key sales skill.

This detached viewpoint is particularly useful if you find yourself being drawn into an argument with a customer or trying to prove a point. You will be stuck in your own perspective and leaning forward, probably hunched over the telephone. You are being sucked into a difficult situation. The moment you become aware of this happening to you, lean back and take a detached point of view. Leaning back breaks the physical involvement in the argument. Then check rapport, acknowledge the customer's viewpoint and summarise to check exactly what the issue is about.

As you talk, summarise regularly, using the customer's words as far as possible, and wait for agreement before proceeding.

'So if I understand you right, you are interested in a three-day communication skills training, beginning in the last quarter of this year, for about 50 of your sales force, and the budget would have to be approved in advance. Is that right?'

ENDING THE CONVERSATION

How do you end a telephone conversation? With words *and* voice. 'Thank you for your time. I won't keep you now, and look forward to meeting/talking to you on...'

As you say this, mismatch the customer's voice. This is the opposite of matching. Speeding up your rate of speech works well. Then both words and voice tone give the same message. If you have trouble getting off the telephone, mismatching is a very effective way to bring the conversation to a natural end.

When do you end a telephone conversation? End the call when you have your goal. If you do not get your goal in that conversation, make sure you have agreed and scheduled a next step – a meeting, another telephone conversation – or arranged for some material to be sent in the post. Never leave a conversation with the customer simply saying he will call you. Ninety per cent of the time he will not. Take responsibility in the initial call for setting up the next contact. If the customer says he will call you in a week, say something like, 'Good. I'll look forward to your call by next Friday. If you are busy and forget, how long shall I leave it before calling again?'

He may say, 'Leave it until the following Tuesday.'

Then say, 'OK. What time suits you best?'

Get a definite arrangement.

When a customer says, 'I'll contact you' and refuses to be pinned down any further, then he is probably not interested, but is not willing to tell you outright. Accept the situation and assume he will not call. Similarly, 'Call me in six months,' is another way of saying, 'Go away,' unless it is backed by good reasons and a definite agreement about calling back on a given date.

You may have been in the unfortunate situation where the customer makes an appointment and then is not there when you keep it. You may have travelled a long way and feel justifiably annoyed. The customer may be downright discourteous or may not be committed. Think back to the telephone call. Perhaps you pushed a bit hard. Perhaps he agreed to an appointment just to appease you. Maybe the conversation was full of you talking and the customer going, 'Uh huh … sure … sure … uh huh.'

Never accept appointments that have not been clearly agreed by both parties. Confirm them in writing, if time allows. If there is a problem, the customer will call you and reschedule because he wants to meet you, not because he feels he has to.

FOLLOW UP CALLS

By the time you are making a follow up call, you know the customer and you have a relationship, however tenuous. However, it is still worth reminding him of your name, company and reason for ringing in your second call.

Refer to your last conversation and what was agreed. Make the reference to something pleasant or interesting. You do not want the customer to associate you with the last time the computers went down or that dreadful day when the pipes burst.

Again, check that this is a good time to speak, as it starts the conversation on the right footing.

'Hello, this is John Jones from XYZ. We spoke last Tuesday about our training course, and about skiing too, I remember.'

'Oh yes. Hello.'

'We agreed I would call you today. Is this a good time to speak?'

Sometimes the customer has not had time to think about your original proposals or read the literature you sent.

If this is the case, say, 'OK, how can we best proceed from here?'

Usually it is best to arrange another call. If you call again and she has still done nothing, be careful. Schedule a third call. Make this the last. Behaviour speaks louder than words and she may not be interested. Be direct here. Directness and honesty are sometimes uncomfortable, but people will respect you for them.

Do not hang onto prospects who demonstrate they are not really interested; do not countenance an elaborate pretence between you.

Say, 'I notice that I've called you a couple of times already. We can't move forward without your thoughts. Is there anything I can do to help? I do not want to waste your time ... or mine [say this under your breath] ... unless you are interested and think we have something that is worth us talking together.'

Now it's her turn. She may say that really on reflection she is not interested, in which case all you have lost is the opportunity to make another fruitless telephone call. Ask for a referral. She owes you something for wasting your time by not being direct. Say, 'I appreciate you do not need our product. Is there anyone in your organisation who may be interested?' Ask for a referral based on your customer profile. You have nothing to lose. Then exit gracefully.

Keeping records

Keep a record for each customer of:

date of call
what was agreed
his main points (*in his exact words* – make a note of these during the conversation or immediately after)
any other interesting points that arose
action you need to take
action customer agreed to take
agreed next contact (day and time)

Secretaries

Here is a familiar scenario. You just know that if you could speak to the project manager of XYZ organisation for only two minutes, even one minute, he would jump at your product. It is just what he has been waiting for, the answer to his prayer. You manage to speak to his secretary or assistant, who promises he will pass on your message, but nothing seems to come of it.

Have you ever been in this situation? Do you view secretaries as malevolent barriers to be outwitted before you can get to the person you want to speak to?

Shift perspective. Work with the secretary rather than against him. He can be your ally. Whoever you speak to, your first outcome must be to establish a relationship. On an initial call, voice match the greeting.

Say, 'This is John Jones of XYZ. I am not sure who I should be talking to. Can I tell you why I am calling, so you can direct me to the right person?'

If the person you need to speak to is the secretary's direct boss, ask to leave a brief message of your name and business and when would be a convenient time to call back. The secretary can help you a great deal, giving you names, work and schedules of people you might need to talk to. Trust that the secretary knows his manager's schedule and work, and will transfer you to the most appropriate person.

As a general rule it is a waste of time leaving messages with the silicon secretaries of the nineties – answer phones.

CUSTOMER SERVICE

Check with existing customers by telephone to find out if all is going well. Customers sometimes suspect that salespeople are only interested in their order. And sometimes they are right. Keep in touch with your customers and listen to what they say. Find out if there is anything else you can do for them or if they have problems.

Giving bad news

Remember the Peter Principle? 'What can go wrong will go wrong, given enough time.' Sooner or later a delivery will be late or faulty, or a course unable to start on time and the customer will be left to deal with the consequences. You may have to convey the news to him. For example:

'Hello, Mr Smith. This is John Jones of XYZ.'

'Hello, how's the order going?'

'Well, there's some bad news I'm afraid and I drew the short straw to tell you.'

'Oh no, a delay?'

'Yes, I'm afraid so. We made a mistake and we are over-committed next month. I would like to reschedule for 5 March. I'm not pleased about that or at having to tell you. What can I do to make it better for you?'

'I don't know. We have all our people ready, I'm going to have to tell them.'

'Can I write you a note, so you can post it to tell them exactly· what's happened?'

'OK.'

'I can promise delivery on 5 March.'

'OK. Can you give me a discount on price to make up for the inconvenience?'

'I am not sure. Perhaps, but I would have to discuss it with my manager first. Can I get back to you on that?'

'All right.'

'Is there anything else I can do to soften the blow?'

'I suppose a life-size effigy of your company president for bonfire night is out of the question?'

'Sorry, yes.'

'All right, write me that letter and let me know about the discount.'

'I will. I'll let you know tomorrow.'

Dealing with complaints

Voice matching is particularly important when giving bad news, and it is crucial when dealing with complaints. Someone who is angry will typically speak faster and louder than usual. *Match that, but slightly below his level.* If you voice match exactly, he may think you are being combative and get even angrier. Voice matching slightly below gives an urgency and edge to your voice, and shows that you are in rapport.

'It broke down again? I don't believe it!
'I'd be furious too. Give me the details and I'll light some fires!'

Do not take complaints personally. Join the customer in his reality. You will not be able to influence him unless you join him first.

When faced with an angry person, we have a natural tendency to talk more softly and placate, but this rarely works. A gentle voice often makes him angrier, as he may think you are not taking him seriously or are being patronising. Once you are matching him, you can gradually lead him down to a more reasoned and reasoning attitude. Then make your goal to find out what went wrong and what you can do to make it right again.

USING THE TELEPHONE

Key Points

- Establish rapport on the telephone by voice matching:
  match the speed and volume of the customer's voice
  match their key words and phrases
- Make a mental picture of the customer in your mind's eye.
- Clear your mind of internal dialogue.
- Keep in a good emotional state.
- Be clear about the purpose of your call.

INITIAL CONTACT
- Voice match.
- Give your name and brief description of what you do.
- Ask if it is a convenient time to speak.

DURING THE CONVERSATION
- Guide the conversation by asking questions.
- Use the three different viewpoints:
  your own
  the customer's
  the detached view
- Summarise regularly and check understanding.

ENDING THE CONVERSATION
- Use your words and your tone to indicate your wish to finish.
- Mismatch the customer's voice.
- Arrange the next stage.

CUSTOMER SERVICE
- Keep records of your conversations
- Establish rapport with secretaries and treat them as allies.
- Dealing with complaints:
  voice match a little below the level of intensity
  gradually soften your voice so the dissatisfied customer calms
  down as well
  gather information so you can work out what to do next

RAPPORT – BUILDING RELATIONSHIPS

6

An experiment was conducted a few years ago. A man approached people in the centre of London and offered them a ten pound note in exchange for a five pound note. Logically, this was a foolproof deal for the passers-by. Yet most of them did not take the ten pound note. Why? It was too good to be true. They did not know or trust the person who was offering them five pounds profit for nothing. They thought it surely must be a trick and a Candid Camera presenter would jump out of the shadows. Most people will not take a winning offer unless they trust the person who is offering it.

So in a face-to-face meeting with the customer the first sales skill is to build a relationship of trust and rapport. Rapport is the soil in which all other skills grow. It is the main missing ingredient in the electronic bazaar. It is the quality that will ensure the future of sales-people irrespective of technology.

Cultural rapport

Rapport operates at many levels and the first is cultural. If you are selling internationally, take care and get to know the culture. For example, while the British value humour and use it in sales meetings, in many European countries making a joke in a meeting would be regarded as stupid.

Large companies, too, have a culture all their own – you need to get to know it if you are to succeed within them.

Then there is cultural image. Within our culture we have said sales-people in general have a poor image. This book seeks to start to change that. Doctors, by contrast, as members of a highly valued profession, do not need to have great rapport skills to be trusted.

Safety

As long as you do not start an argumentative discussion about controversial topics like religion or politics, you are hardly likely to pose a personal threat to the customer. Your product may. When you are making a big sale, you may destabilise vested interests. Ironically, the better your product, the greater the threat. Buying represents change and many people feel threatened by change.

One way to minimise change is to set boundaries around the change, run a trial in one department, for example. Another way is to dwell on how your product or service enables customers to do what they have always done, only *better*. A new computer system may be completely different but it will do the *same* work faster.

Training and consulting are sold on increased personal, departmental and organisational performance. Show what stays the same as well as what will change. While some people like radical change and others like everything to stay the same, most people feel comfortable with a mixture.

Personal rapport

Personal rapport is building mutual trust in a face-to-face meeting. We communicate and influence people through three main channels: our body language, our voice tone and the words we use.

Rapport is established and maintained by matching these three aspects. People like people who are like themselves. Creating a relationship of trust and believability through matching body language is a learnable and natural skill, and the best communicators in every profession do it. In sales, management, medicine and education, rapport building through matching is a consistent pattern of top performers.

BODY LANGUAGE

Appearance

The first noticeable aspect of body language is your dress and appearance. Dressing to be accepted in a business culture is one way of matching that culture. We form impressions of others in a very short time, less than 10 seconds, and base these early impressions mostly on dress and appearance. No one is aware of precisely what personal judgements and prejudices are brought to bear in those first few seconds. Some people make such quick, rigid judgements that only a middle-aged, white Anglo Saxon male, with short hair, wearing an expensive suit and shoes will get the full seal of approval. This type of executive, in a straitjacket of his own making, may be unaware that he has inflicted these blinkers on himself.

Do not let habit take over how you dress and groom – be smart and fit into the culture you have to enter. Blend the style of the culture into which you are selling with your personal style and preferences. Your appearance communicates how you feel about yourself. By accepting yourself, you make it more likely that others will accept you too. If you are still rejected prematurely and unfairly, remember that it is not you who is lacking, but the other person's world that is too narrow for you to enter.

Posture and movement

The second way we gain rapport is to match posture and movements. The next time you are in a gathering where people are talking, look round and notice who you think are getting on well with each other and who are not. One intuitive way of knowing this is the degree to which we see their body language match.

Some body language matching is obvious. If a customer is sitting down, so do we; if they stand, it feels more comfortable to stand too. If the other person is making a lot of gestures, you may find it an effort to stay still. You can match general posture. You can match head nods and weight shifts.

A lot of eye contact will not necessarily get you rapport. Initiate the same amount of eye contact as the customer, the amount *she* is comfortable with.

Confine your body language matching to general posture, speed of gesture and amount of eye contact. Match over time and not simultaneously. You can also cross match, which means matching with a different part of your body. For example, if the client is swinging his leg, do not do the same, but maybe move your hand at the same rate.

Remember, matching is not mimicry. Mimicry is overt and exact copying of the other person's behaviour and will have quite the opposite effect to the one you are seeking.

Part of body language is the way we use space. We all need personal space around us and feel uncomfortable if this is breached without permission. In European culture this personal space extends about 18 inches all round us when standing. People will move away imperceptibly when you breach that barrier. Be sensitive to this.

If you are negotiating with a customer, it helps to move beside him so you can look at the issues in a more co-operative and detached way. Write the issues to be dealt with on a flip chart on the other side of the room, walk over, sit beside the client and ask, 'How can *we* solve this?'

Matching works – use it well

Matching body language is like creating a dance. Partners do not exactly copy each other's movements but make them complementary. A good example of this is cross over matching. This is when you match the other person's body language with a different type of movement. For example, instead of crossing your legs when he does, you could fold your arms. Moving your hand in time with his speech rhythm is another example. Matching body language is a natural human expression of interest. It is one way, and a powerful one, of creating rapport. When you first experiment with matching, you may feel awkward. This is because you are becoming aware of what you are doing naturally anyway, but now you are gaining choice about when and how much you do it. Like doing up your shoelaces, it works best when you do not think about it.

Two words of caution. First, start by practising in safe situations, with family, friends and colleagues, before you use matching consciously with customers. Secondly, creating rapport, of which body matching is one aspect, flows from a sincere interest in the customer and desire to know him. Matching body language will feel *and look* uncomfortable and phony if you do it as a technique to influence customers you have no interest in and do not really want to talk to. It will feel and appear hollow and contrived. Rapport is not a sales technique to 'do' to customers. It is a powerful way of entering their world and getting to know them better.

What does body language mean?

In general, nothing by itself. A particular customer's movements and gestures will have a definite meaning *which you cannot know in advance.* Some schools of thought suggest that certain postures or gestures always have the same meaning. For example, we have read that when a customer folds his arms, he is not interested, a customer who leans back is withdrawing, rubbing the side of his nose means he is lying, etc. This is not so. You cannot realistically say that a gesture always means the same thing regardless of who is doing it. You need to watch what your particular customer does. When he is interested, he may lean forward. When you have seen him do this two or three times, then you can assume the connection. Another customer may lean back when he is interested. A third customer may indeed rub his nose when he lies and a fourth may rub his nose because he suffers from hay fever. The words people say and the gestures they make are individual and personal. Making sense of specific gestures for particular customers is called *calibration* in NLP and demands careful observation, not remembering a set list of features.

SPEECH

Voice tone

Voice tone is the second most important channel of communication. We have already talked about matching voice tone to establish rapport on the telephone. Matching the speed and volume of the customer's voice works just as well in face-to-face meetings.

Pacing and leading

Matching is one example of what is called *pacing* in NLP. Pacing is joining the other person in her world, appreciating her view. Matching body language and voice tone is pacing at a non-verbal level. Pacing is like walking with a person at the same speed while you talk together. Falling behind or getting too far ahead stops the conversation.

You are taking the initiative, so it is for you to pace the customer. Once you are pacing him, you can slow down slightly or speed up your pace and, if you have good rapport, he will follow. This is *leading*.

One example of this which we have already seen is voice matching an angry customer at a slightly lower level and then gradually lowering your voice. If you have rapport, he will follow into a more reasoned state. In the same way, when you show a customer you have heard and appreciate what he says by using his own words when you check for agreement, he will be more amenable to discussion. Understanding his point of view does not mean however that you have to agree with it.

Anytime you do not know what to do next in a sales meeting, simply turn your attention to pacing the customer's body language and voice. Let her lead you for a moment. Once you know where she is going, you will know what to say.

Words

Words are important, yet not as important as we think. This is backed by research that found that people tend to hear only about 50 per cent of what you say and retain about 10 per cent of that. So they hear and retain 5 per cent of your words. This is why we give less attention to scripts in this book than in most sales books. More important than words themselves is how you say them and what you do while saying them.

If your customer is going to remember such a small part of what you say, decide for yourself in advance what you want him to remember. Put crucial facts in writing.

We tend to best remember what happens at the beginning and the end of meetings, so give your important messages then. Use your voice to *emphasise* what you want the customer to remember. *Mark it out* with

a gesture as well, to reinforce the message. Do this consistently and use the same gesture to mark out the point when you repeat it. This leads us on to the next point...

Listening and backtracking

We have already mentioned backtracking: using the same key words as the customer in your discussion. We will expand on it now, as it is an important skill.

First, backtracking is audible evidence for the customer that you are listening. When he knows you are listening, this builds rapport. How will you know his key words? He will *emphasise* them with his voice. And perhaps *mark them out* with a gesture. Exactly as you will be doing, but unawares. Listen for those words. Listen to exactly how he expresses what he wants and needs. Listen to what is important to him. When you backtrack, mark out the key words in the same way as the customer.

Some salespeople will check back with the customer by paraphrasing his words. But words mean different things to different people and if you paraphrase, you translate into your meaning. You may use a word, which, although it has exactly the same meaning for you, does not work for the customer. So paraphrasing usually means distorting.

An example:

Customer: 'I want this training course to *motivate* and *empower* the people on it. Let's work out some details of how you can do this... I want them to be able to take away *course materials,* so we need to talk about how these will be distributed ... and I believe that *free discussion* groups are really useful in a training like this. The last training that we had missed these out and I think the training suffered as a result.'

Salesperson: 'Good. We will make this course really powerful and inspirational. There will be handouts throughout ... and we will make sure there are brainstorming sessions built in.'

Customer: 'No. That's not what I want at all.'

A backtrack would go as follows:

Salesperson: 'Good, I gather you want this course to be *motivating* and *empowering*. You want them to have *course materials* to take away ... and be able to participate in *free discussion* groups.'

Customer: 'Exactly.'

Backtracking helps to establish rapport and agreement. Never assume you understand what the customer means. She lives in a different world.

Once you have the key words, you need to translate them into words and actions you can understand. In our example, the salesperson would go on to ask questions like:

> 'Can you give me an idea or an example of a training that is motivating and empowering?'
> 'How would you evaluate whether it was both motivating and empowering?'

These questions start to unpack those key words 'motivating' and 'empowering' so you can share the customer's understanding and criteria. To go on to 'course materials' and 'free discussions':

> 'What course materials did you have in mind?' (Handouts might be far from her mind.)
> 'Tell me about the free discussions that will add to the sessions. How would they work?'

Backtracking has many benefits:

- *Checking for agreement.* Backtracking establishes points of agreement with the customer.

- *Building and demonstrating rapport.* The customer's key words describe what is important to her, so you are acknowledging these and demonstrating that you have been listening with attention.

- *Surfacing and reducing misunderstandings.* When you backtrack, you will discover areas where you are uncertain. So you can then ask questions to clarify the meaning. Sometimes when you backtrack, a customer may say, 'Well, yes ... but come to think about it, that is not exactly what I want.' So it can clarify things for the customer as well.

- *Moving the meeting on.* Backtracking is like punctuation in a sentence. It signals a pause, a review, before moving forward.

Words to avoid

But

'But' is a word that disempowers the part of the sentence that precedes it. For example:

> 'You say it's expensive, but look at the benefits the product gives...'
> 'You are doing well already, but I can show you how to do better...'
> 'I know you are busy, but I am sure you will like to see this product...'

Replacing 'but' with 'and' keeps the link and does not cancel, disqualify or cast doubt on the first part of the sentence. You can nearly always rephrase the sentence more positively.

So, 'I know immediate delivery is important, but we can't get it to you until Friday' becomes 'I know early delivery is important to you and we can guarantee delivery by Friday.'

The moment many people hear 'but' they stop listening to what follows, because they are too busy thinking about defending what was wrong.

Try

Try and avoid the word 'try'. Try really hard. Notice that the word 'try' implies difficulty, even impossibility. The harder you try the more difficult it becomes. If you ask someone to do you a favour and he says, 'I'll try', do you think he will or not? Sales is about opening possibilities, not suggesting problems.

Do this experiment. Put your pen on the floor and try to pick it up. You are not allowed to actually pick it up, because then you will not be trying any more, you will be *succeeding*.

Rather than say 'I'll try' to requests, give a straight 'Yes' or 'No' or 'Perhaps.' The Peter Principle states that everything that can go wrong will go wrong if you wait long enough, so be aware of this. Discuss problems.

Negatives

Customers will often tell you what they do not want:

'I don't want a carpet like the last one, it fell to pieces within a year.'
'I don't want to be kept waiting for delivery.'

This can be useful, because it tells you what is important for them to avoid. It gives the 'away from' part of the need, although this is only half the story. You still need to know what they want instead, the other half. Ask about what sort of carpet they want and when they actually want delivery.

In your own talk it is best to avoid negatives. For example, there is the classic phrase, 'I don't want to be difficult.' You just know this will be followed by a 'but...' and then something that is difficult. Denying it in advance just makes it more obvious. Better to say, 'I foresee a possible difficulty here that you might help me with.'

Think about this example: 'Don't *worry* about delivery, there is no reason why we cannot supply it by next week.'

This is actually an invitation to worry and to begin to imagine reasons why it will not arrive by next week.

Negatively phrased sentences actually act as a command on a deeper level. To say, 'Don't worry,' is an instruction to notice problems, worry or do whatever you are asked not to do.

If I ask you not to think of your greatest competitor, what happens? You must think of them in order to understand the sentence. How do you not think of something? Only by thinking of something else. So think of your best customer. Phrase in the positive. 'Be assured...' rather than 'Don't worry...'

We do not want you to think of all the possible things that could go wrong with the sale if you did not stop using negatives.

Was this last sentence clear?

Negatives can also be confusing, can they not?

RAPPORT

Key Points

- The first sales skill is to build a relationship of trust and rapport with your customer.
- There are three levels of rapport:
  Cultural. This is how salespeople are perceived in general.
  Safety. This is whether a person feels threatened by a salesperson or her product.

Personal. This is building mutual trust and influence in a face-to-face meeting.

- Establish and maintain rapport by matching:

    Body language:

    dress appropriately

    match general posture, amount and speed of gesture and amount of eye contact

    Speech:

    match voice tone

    mark out your important points

    backtrack using the same key words as the customer

    replace 'but' with 'and'

    avoid the word 'try'

    phrase in the positive

- Practise matching in safe situations.
- Make it an expression of your sincere interest.
- Matching is an example of pacing: joining the other person in his world.

SPEAKING THE CUSTOMER'S LANGUAGE

7

Building rapport is the first step in selling. You establish a connection with the customer where you are both open to influence. Once you have established rapport, what then?

Your aim is to identify what the customer wants and what is important to him because you are looking to match his need, buying criteria and priorities with your product and the standards of your company. To identify whether or not this match exists, you need to know what and how the customer thinks.

How do you find out *what* and *how* somebody thinks? Surely that information is locked away in people's heads? Yet, as you listen, the customer's words will tell you not only what he thinks but *how* he thinks. And when you know how he thinks, you can explain and discuss his need and your products in the way he is most likely to understand. We have already said that the same words mean different things to different people. This section will give you an insight into your customer's mind, so you can pick the right words to use – the ones *he* will respond to.

WAYS OF THINKING

Think back to your last successful sales meeting. Take a few moments to remember it, so you could describe it to yourself...

What did you do? How did you remember it? You may have visualised the scene and the client. You may have heard the sounds and voices again in your mind. You probably felt good about the result and may have talked to yourself about it. We take information in from the world with our five senses: visual, auditory, feeling, taste and smell. Then we re-experience it, that is, we *re-present* parts of it to ourselves when we think.

NLP takes the five senses – visual, auditory, kinesthetic (feeling), olfactory (smell) and gustatory (taste) – and examines how we use them internally to think, calling them *representational* systems. Thinking is a mixture of the five representational systems. But we don't all do it the same way. Some people are more aware of the internal pictures they make in their visual system. Others talk to themselves a great deal and use the auditory system more. Many people are most aware of their feelings and body sensations (the kinesthetic system).

As already mentioned, how we think is reflected in what we say. People who are thinking in pictures will use words such as 'see', 'perspective', 'look', 'bright', 'vision' and 'scene'. They may use phrases like 'I'm glad we see eye to eye' or 'That's too vague, I need to see it in black and white.'

A person who is thinking in sounds or hearing an internal voice will use words like 'say', 'tell', 'question', 'speak', 'tune' and 'demand'. She may use phrases like 'I hear you loud and clear.' She will 'talk things over' or 'listen to your proposal'. She may say, 'It seems a good idea but something tells me it won't work.'

A person who thinks using feelings will use words like 'touch', 'move', 'grasp', 'feel', 'smooth', 'solid', 'firm' and 'balance'. He is likely to use such phrases as 'It's been weighing on my mind' or 'She's a cool customer.' They will 'touch upon' topics or 'carry the project through'.

These words that refer to one of our senses are known as *predicates* in NLP.

There are also many words that we use that are not specific to any sense. Words like 'prove', 'discover', 'allow', 'think', 'plan', 'know', 'motivate' and 'believe' give no clue about seeing, hearing and feeling.

Here are some common words or phrases you might use, 'translated' across systems to show you how it sounds, so you can get a feel for it:

Neutral	Visual	Auditory	Kinesthetic
consider the idea	look into it	sound it out	explore
demonstrate the product	show you	explain it to you	give you a feel for it
discuss	look over	talk over	go over
remind you	show you again	recall	take you back
I understand.	I see what you are saying.	I hear you loud and clear.	I can grasp the point you are putting over.

Neutral	Visual	Auditory	Kinesthetic
I don't understand.	That's not clear.	That sounds odd.	That doesn't fit.
I know.	That's clear to me.	Sounds right.	I get a sense of that.

Listen – respond – use

Now you know what to listen for, the next step is to hear what your customers say and notice when they use sensory-based words. After a few days you will start to see, hear and sense all of them more easily. Once you can do that, you can begin to match them in your response.

Although we all use all the different ways of thinking all the time, when you pay attention to the predicates people use, you may find some people tend to use more visual expressions, others more feeling expressions, others more auditory expressions. When you know which system they favour, you too can start to express yourself in that system, because people like people who think in the same way as they do.

Try this experiment. Recommend a film you have seen to a friend or colleague in the following three different ways to find out which one was most persuasive.

First: 'The film was really good. The photography was brilliant. You really got a deep insight into the main characters' minds. The images were memorable, I would love to see it again.'

Second: 'What a strong film that was! Really powerful characterisation that held your attention. The feelings of the characters really came over. Go and see it whatever you do. It's a hit. You will be riveted to the screen.'

Third: 'I've got to tell you about this film. Marvellous dialogue and a terrific soundtrack. The motives of the principal characters came over loud and clear. I like a film that tells a cracking good story.'

The first description was visual, the second kinesthetic and the third auditory. These are exaggerated examples and they make it easy to see, hear and feel how you can say the same thing in different ways. Your message is the same, but a friend may not feel motivated to see the first film, yet want to see the second. (But remember – it's the *same film.*) Think what a difference this could make when you describe your product.

To find out your own preferred way of thinking and expressing

yourself, talk for five minutes about your work into a tape recorder·
without tracking what you are saying. Then go back over what you
recorded and note the different types of words. Notice whether your
language has a predominance of one or two of the different ways of
thinking.

You might then notice that if you tend to think in pictures, you get
good rapport and probably better results with customers who also
think in pictures. You may be less effective with customers who think
in feelings. Food for thought – to use a gustatory phrase.

Technical words and jargon

Using the customer's language will build rapport and translate the
features and benefits of your product for him in the way he is most
comfortable with. When doing this, use the customer's technical
vocabulary, if he does. All business has its jargon and these words
concentrate a lot of meaning for the customer. Using the jargon is not
about trying to impress the customer and pretending you know the
words. It is about using his vocabulary to match his way of thinking.
Ask what the words mean if you have not already done your home-
work, get his translation, then use them when you feel confident to do
so. And avoid your own sales jargon.

Thinking and speed of speech

Words are one way these different ways of thinking manifest themselves. There are others. Imagine thinking in pictures. Pictures happen
quickly and have a lot of information in them all at once. People who
think a lot in pictures – and you may be one yourself – tend to talk
quickly to keep up with the pictures. Thinking in feelings is usually
slower, because feelings need time.

So a visual thinker talking to a feeling thinker can be a disastrous
mismatch. The visual thinker will be talking fast, saying things like,
'Come and look at this proposal. I've sketched out a few ideas here to
put your problem into perspective.'

The feeling thinker will be talking more slowly, saying things like, 'I
don't feel entirely comfortable with this plan yet. I get a sense of some
gaps. Let's not grab too quickly at the easy solution.'

Once you develop an ear for dialogue, its value becomes obvious.
It is not so much what people say – although of course this is important too – it is the way they say it.

Figures of speech

As we have seen, given that people think in different ways, they will use different phrases which you can match.

You can also make up your own phrases within the same representational system. Here are some examples:

Visual

'I see what you mean.'
'Let me shed some light on the matter.'
'Beyond a shadow of a doubt.'
'The future looks bright.'
'I want to get this problem into a sharp focus.'

Auditory

'That rings a bell.'
'I hear what you are saying.'
'In a manner of speaking.'
'This is unheard of.'
'I can't hear myself think.'

Kinesthetic

'I'll be in touch with you.'
'Hold on a second.'
'I can't put my finger on it.'
'That's a firm foundation to the proposal.'
'I have a solid grasp of the main points.'

Suppose a customer says, 'I foresee difficulties. Can you *show* me a way around that problem?'

A good reply would be, 'Sure, let me sketch out some possibilities to see which looks best to you.'

Then you could literally draw some of the options on a flip chart if you are doing a presentation, or on a piece of paper.

A reply that went, 'Sure, let me walk you through the possibilities to give you a good grasp of the choice available,' would not match the way the customer expressed the reservation, for it uses feeling and action words and does not match the customer's visual thinking.

Another customer might say, 'That *sounds* difficult. It doesn't *ring* true to me yet.'

She seems to be hearing the difficulty.

Your reply: 'Let's try and fine tune the proposal. I can say a lot more about it.'

Then talk about it, do not use diagrams.

A third customer: 'I feel there is a block here. How can I steer clear of the issue?'

So: 'Let me guide you through the steps, so you can get clear of this.'

You will still have to deal with the objection of course, but you have let her know you understand her thinking.

Metaphors

We can expand the idea of matching phrases and figures of speech by including the use of stories and analogies that are drawn from the customer's interests and work.

For example, financial planning for an athlete might mean talking about different policies being like different athletic events, some built for stamina, taking longer, others built for speed, but without the same staying power. For a musician, it would involve getting all the different parts of her life in harmony. NLP uses the word *metaphor* to describe stories and figures of speech that involve a comparison. They can illuminate a subject and make it memorable, like taking somebody to view the sun setting on the horizon in order to talk about the future.

If I were a brick-layer teaching someone how to build a wall, one thing I could do would be demonstrate how to lay a brick. If I were a parent hoping to shape a child's behaviour, the best thing I could do would be to behave the way I wanted the child to behave. If I were an officer in the army intent on having his troops charge the enemy, the best thing I could do would be to lead the charge. So I'll give some more examples.

I was talking to the Managing Director of a company who was experiencing terrible problems with his Board of Directors. The Directors were far more concerned about their personal goals than they were about the corporate goals. A great deal of their time was spent politicking, putting each other down and trying to undermine each other's authority. The job of running the business was becoming incidental.

I said to the Managing Director, 'I've got this picture of Charlton

Heston in *Ben Hur*. You're on your chariot and you're battling to win the race but all your horses are pulling in different directions and you're about to be overtaken.'

'That's it,' the Managing Director said with some relief because not only had I demonstrated, and therefore shared, an understanding of his problem, I had also clarified his experience and his feelings.

Another example was a stationery supply company who were losing customers due to late and inaccurate deliveries. The sales side of the company was excellent but growing disillusioned by the failure of the company to hold onto customers. The quality of the products was second to none.

'So,' I said to the Managing Director, 'deliveries are a bit like the holes in a rain barrel that are stopping it filling up.'

'Yes, they are. Can you help me plug the holes?' she asked.

On another occasion I was talking to someone who had set up a number of estate agencies and recruited, at great expense, top negotiators from other agencies, only to find they were not performing.

'So,' I said, 'you're a football manager with money to spend. You've bought the best players. But where's the captain who's going to get the best out of them? Where are the training sessions? And who's going to tell them what style of play is wanted?'

He nodded knowingly and we worked together on a plan that resulted in recruiting a sales manager who introduced company standards and a training programme.

Tangible and intangible benefits

Products are often tangible. A car can be touched, sat in and driven. A fax machine can send and receive messages that can be read. However, the benefits that products afford may be less tangible in some instances. The general advantages that are derived can be understood. The specific benefits to the individual customer may be less easily defined.

Imagine that I'm an author working on a typewriter. The worst thing about my current or problem state is that my work needs a great deal of revision and correction and that means typing the work over again. The implications of this are that I spend longer than I need to on my work, miss deadlines and have to turn down other work. A demonstration of a word processor would be a powerful sales argument in its own right. However, imagine the salesperson saying, 'This word processor has the ability to make corrections to existing text and then print out the revised document without duplication of the work that can remain unaltered. For you, this means that there will be no more wasted time, missed deadlines or refused work.'

It's a powerful case that has proven to be true and value for money. However, take yourself back to the early days of word processors when the case for them had still to be proven and their cost, compared to other office equipment, was far higher than it is now. Add to the sales-person's benefit description, 'You would be like a brick-layer who, finding his wall had gone out of line, could simply run his hand along it to straighten it rather than knock it down and start again.' That metaphor conveys the ease of the 'new' compared to the labour of the 'old' and summarises the benefits.

Training and development of staff can seem like an avoidable 'cost' to some companies. This is often because the results and benefits of spending the money to train staff are difficult to measure and quantify. The cost of training may be high, but the cost of ignorance is usually higher. How can you put this across?

In Canada they held the world lumberjack championships. The two finalists were deadly enemies. Each was allocated an equal section of forest and they began to cut into the trees. After an hour, lumberjack Joe heard lumberjack Fred stop cutting. So lumberjack Joe cut into his trees with greater energy to take advantage of this pause in Fred's work. Ten minutes later, Fred started up again.

The pause in Fred's activity occurred every hour of the five-hour competition. Joe, understandably, thought he had won easily. After all, he had heard Fred stop cutting for ten minutes every hour. To his surprise, when the final count was taken, Joe had lost. Dejected and disillusioned, he sought an explanation. He asked Fred how he had managed to cut so many trees *and* stop to rest every hour.

'I wasn't resting,' Fred said, 'just sharpening my axe.'

SPEAKING THE CUSTOMER'S LANGUAGE

Key Points

- Thinking is a mixture of:
  internal pictures (visual representation system)
  internal sounds and self-talk (auditory representation system)
  internal feelings (kinesthetic representation system)

- We choose our words and phrases according to how we are thinking.
- Use words and phrases drawn from the customer's way of thinking to enhance rapport and respond most effectively.
- Use longer metaphors and figures of speech drawn from the customer's interests.

VALUES, RULES AND DECISION STRATEGIES

What does the customer want?

There is a present problem and a better future in every need. Present trouble is usually more compelling than a better future simply because it is here and now. So, when a customer is reasonably happy in the present and is focusing more on moving towards a better future, direct his attention to what is wrong now. Develop dissatisfaction with the present. Movement needs either a pull or a push. But both at once works best of all. To explore futures, ask questions like,

'What will it be like to have solved this problem?'
'What will you have then that you do not have now?'

To focus on present dissatisfaction, ask questions like:

'What are the implications for your business if this present situation goes unchecked?'

To focus on both problems and solutions, ask:

'What are the benefits and drawbacks of the current situation?'

Whatever level of management, there will be both a personal and organisational side to the present problem and desired future.

For example, suppose you are selling yourself as a consultant to an organisation and are approaching the client company using a 'middle up' strategy. The personal benefit for your initial contact could be promotion. If you solve the problem, he takes the credit for using you. His personal problem may be that he is spending long hours at work. The consequent benefit could be he gets more time with his family and feels less stressed.

There will also be a business problem and a business benefit. The business problem may be that productivity is low, or morale is bad in his department, or the department is not keeping within its budget. The business benefit may be the smooth running of his department, contributing to the overall profitability of the company. Business gets results and individuals win.

Personal benefit:
Promotion

Personal away from:
Long working hours

Business benefit:
Smooth performance

Business away from:
Low morale
Low productivity
Exceeding budgets

Moving from need to solution

When you are selling advisory or consulting skills, clients may have a good idea of what their need is in general terms, but not how to meet it. For example, I know I want to save money, but I am not sure how or how much. Or I want a greater focus on customer service in my company. How do I get it? *This is moving down from a general need to a specific solution.*

Other times, customers may be clear exactly what they want and only one solution will do. They want a particular savings plan, a particular sales course. This is where you can use your skill and knowledge to explore whether there are other possibilities that would meet the need better than the solution the client has already decided on. She may not have all the facts or there may be an even better way for her of solving her problem. Here you will be *moving up from a specific solution to the general need* to discover whether there is a better solution to that general need.

Here is an example. Suppose you are a consultant and a manager tells you, 'I want a three-day training course at no more than £600 a day to begin no later than the first of next month.' This is very specific. Whether you can supply this or not, explore the need to which this is a solution. Ask questions like, 'What do you want the training course to do?' The answer may be to increase productivity in a particular department. That being so, there are other possibilities such as computer assisted learning or consultancy. There is also the option of a skills modelling project to find out what the most productive people in the company currently do differently from those less successful and then design a training course to teach the others how to work that way. Any of these may be a better way of increasing productivity than running a three-day training course.

Another question you would ask is, 'What is important about £600 a day as a ceiling?' Perhaps there is a total budget of £1,800, which also explains why it is to be a three-day course. The £1,800 does not have necessarily to fund a three-day training course, however. It has to fund a solution.

A third question: 'What would happen if it started later than the first of next month?' It may be that key workers will be involved in another project after that date. You can explore whether it is possible to defer the projects or work round them.

This is an example of taking details and moving up to the wider need, then finding other ways to satisfy that need. You move up from a single requirement to a need that is broad enough to encompass different solutions – a general principle that can be used for selling anything from consultancy to office furniture.

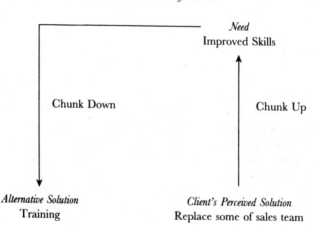

Problem: Low Sales Performance

Figure 7 Moving up and moving down

VALUES AND CRITERIA

What is important?

Whichever way you move, towards or away from, you will need to find out what is important to the customer. These basic issues are known as *criteria* and *values* in NLP. Values are the bigger chunk – what is important to us overall. Very often they are emotional states and are the driving forces behind everything we do. Examples of these values are good health, love, prestige, fun, power, success and learning.

A salesperson we know started selling cars in the late sixties. Having an eye to the future, he asked others in the business which manufacturers were likely to be the main players in the industry over the next two decades. To his surprise, bearing in mind we are going back many years, he was not recommended German, British or American cars. He was told that Japan was going to be the great car manufacturing nation. Consequently, he joined a company who had a franchise for Japanese cars. He honed his sales approach, learnt all about the different models of car available, their reliability, delivery times, etc. He was so impressed by the quality of product he had to sell, he could not envisage failure. And yet, fairly often he would qualify a customer (check she had the need), find out what other makes and models she was looking at, do a performance and cost comparison, and ask for the order. The sales he lost baffled him because he could always at least match, if not beat, other cars on the level of performance, reliability, features and cost. What it took him years to understand was that for many customers there was an unstated value, often unconsciously held, that the car they bought had to be British, even if they were getting less product for money by so doing.

Criteria are less general and wide-ranging than values: they are values applied to a particular context. We use criteria to judge how we fulfil a need. Examples of criteria are cost, time, safety and speed. Cost in money terms is obviously an important criterion. Think of money primarily as a *measure of importance* rather than a criterion in itself.

Everything else being equal, customers will go for the cheapest, but rarely is everything else equal. Your job as salesperson is to point out what is different between what you offer and what your competitor offers. When customers go for the cheapest product or service it may be that they are unaware of their own other more important criteria. So they might as well go for the cheapest. In the last analysis, *you* are the difference.

Both values and criteria are towards a positive or away from a negative. A person may want security for her family. She might think of this primarily as a feeling of safety – or primarily as not feeling threatened. One implies the other and a person will tend to focus more on one side of the equation. Where one person sees peace of mind in a pension plan, another sees not needing to worry any more. You are selling perceived value.

There are some key questions you can use to uncover and explore a customer's criteria. These are probably the most important questions in sales. You would phrase them slightly differently depending on what you are selling:

'What do you want in a [house, holiday, computer, training course]*?'*
'What is most important to you about a [house, holiday, computer, training course]*?'*
'What would having a [house, holiday, computer, training course] *do for you?'*

When you get the customer's criteria, use the same words back to him. If he wants reliability, use 'reliability' in your next question. Do not use 'dependability' or 'trustworthiness', even though these may mean the same to you. You can bet they do not mean the same to the customer.

RULES FOR MEETING CRITERIA

What do criteria mean to you?

Once you have the criteria, you have to find out what they mean to the customer.

For example, a customer tells me he wants 'reliability in a computer'. That is one of his criteria. I have no idea what it means. I have to ask, *'What does reliability in a computer mean to you?'*

He may say, 'The computer must not break down for at least three years.'

This is what has to happen for the product to fulfil his criteria. These requirements are called *criterial equivalents* in NLP. 'Rules for fulfilling his criteria' is another way of thinking about this. When you have these rules or equivalents, you can begin matching them with product features and benefits. The more features of your product you can link to customer criteria the more the customer will be attracted to it.

Other questions that will get rules are:

'How would you decide whether a computer were reliable?'
'How would you know if a computer were reliable – what would it do and what wouldn't it do?'
'What are the qualities of a reliable computer?'
'What evidence do you look for that lets you know it is reliable?'

A salesman of high quality kitchen interiors spent hours discussing the needs of a particular customer, viewing the entire range, measuring and costing out different permutations of lay-out, until the customer finally committed herself to spending many thousands of pounds on a top of the range kitchen. Delivery and installation were arranged. The salesman took great care to brief the installation crew on how to behave and how to handle the customer to make sure that the sale was not in jeopardy. On the afternoon of the installation, he called to check everything was all right, only to find that nothing was going on. There was no sign of the new kitchen. All the customer would say

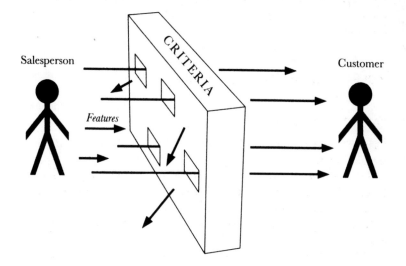

Figure 8 Criteria as filters

before she shut the door was that she was not happy with it after all and had sent it back. The salesman was baffled. The installation crew were baffled; they had done nothing wrong. Management were furious. Fortunately, a few days later the customer phoned to reinstate her order on the strict proviso that it must be delivered in a van clearly painted with the company name and logo, not the plain white van the company had hired for the day to meet a shortage of transportation. It was evident that this customer did not only want to buy the best, she wanted to be seen by her neighbours as buying the best.

When your product matches the customer's criteria and meets the rules, you will have a sale. Typically your product or service will meet some criteria and not others. If you cannot meet them all, of course, it may be that no one else can. A perfect match is then not available to this particular customer. He will then need to compromise, prioritise his criteria. So, reinforce those criteria you can meet, be clear about them and make sure the customer is clear about them. For example, if your fax services are well within your customer's budget and available 24 hours a day, as he wanted, then keep those features to the fore.

Criteria can be expressed in soft or hard measurements. Hard measurements can be measured objectively: a definite budget, a fixed number, a definite date. Soft criteria are a matter of judgement: more user friendly, better looking.

Criteria are not logical, they are emotional, so do not minimise them or argue with them. They cannot be influenced by argument. You can, however, change what they mean. This is called *reframing*. It does not matter whether the criteria are soft or hard. Reframing asks the question: '*What else could this mean?*'

For example, a customer wants a course to start within the next week. If this is not possible for you, reframe it. If it starts within the next week it *could* mean that his people will be unprepared or will not have time to do the pre-course reading. Stress that aspect. Likewise, a customer wants a more complex piece of software – but that *could* mean higher training costs and longer training time. A fax machine with a high transmission and receiving rate *may* risk being incompatible with other machines.

In this way, if you can't meet the criteria, you can point out hidden disadvantages of the criteria being met that the customer may not have considered.

A good example of reframing is in the selling profession generally, where people call themselves 'marketing consultants', rather than 'salespeople', because of the cultural bias against the word 'sales' in the Old Bazaar.

If we refer back to the lady buying the expensive kitchen who rejected delivery in a plain van, we could have reframed the plain van as way of demonstrating just how wealthy she was, because she had no need to flaunt her wealth.

When you cannot reframe criteria, you will need to create alternative solutions to the customer's need. Sometimes you can alter your product to meet criteria. The motor-car industry is very skilful at adapting its products to meet varying criteria. Many people ordering company cars have, apart from obvious, definable needs, criteria such as 'I want to show I'm an individual' or 'I want to show I've been promoted.' All of these personal criteria may be accommodated by buying some of the many 'add ons' available.

COMPETITORS

If we were to ask you to think of your competitors, you might think of other organisations who sell the same or similar products. Competitors are more than these. They are alternative solutions to the same problem *that you are not selling.* If you sell services like training or consultancy, there are many competitor companies supplying such services. However, doing nothing is also a competitive solution for the customer.

Competitor companies

When competing with a company similar to you own, you have two choices and it is best to use them both:

- *Strengthen your own position.*
  Be clear about your own product, how it is different from that of your competitors and where it is the same, with reference to meeting the customer's criteria. Get references from other satisfied customers.

- *Weaken the competition.*
  It is not a good idea to put down the competitor. Customers generally do not like sniping, it diminishes your credibility and actually draws attention to the competition. A better way is to know your competitor's products and give reasons why their product features will not meet the customer's need and criteria.
  When the customer expresses an interest in your competitor's features, ask questions like: 'How do you think that would work out given that [give example of customer's criteria or need]?' This paces the customer's statement and leads him to discover the drawbacks of the competition for himself. These drawbacks will be much more compelling than any you suggest.

Finally, remember your greatest asset – yourself. You add value to the product through your rapport with the customer, your presence, your commitment and your sense of self. Customers buy this in a real sense as well as the product. You are the strongest, the most immediate and most significant reference for your product.

DECISION STRATEGIES

Another question that will also get criteria is:

'What factors influenced your decision to buy your last [product]?'

This question also brings us on to how customers make decisions. People buy in the same way as they bought before – so find out how they bought before.

As a first step, find out whether they were satisfied with how they bought before, particularly if you are selling intangibles like consultancy or training.

Ask questions like:

'Have you done a similar project before?'
'If so, was it successful?'
'What do you attribute the success to?'

If it failed, ask, 'What prevented it from succeeding?'

Find out as much as you can about past decisions for similar products. If the customer is dissatisfied, discover what went wrong. It is always rewarding to learn from the mistakes of others.

Given that the decision was a good one, you now need the strategy the customer used to make the decision to buy. When you know this you can present your product in a way that makes it easy for your customer to decide. Rather like a jigsaw puzzle, all the pieces may be there, but they need organising into a coherent picture.

Making the final decision

No one decides to buy unless the product matches their criteria. Customers take what you say and create the experience of having the product in their minds by a mixture of internal sights, sounds and feelings. If it matches, they buy. If it does not or they are in doubt, they will not buy. This is true whether they are buying training or a book.

The key question to ask here is: *'How will you decide whether this* [product] *is for you?'*

If the customer says, 'Why do you ask?', tell her. You want to know what is important to her and how she decides, so neither of you wastes time.

At this point, the customer may say, 'I don't know, I just decide.' Here you look to her body language for the answer.

Eye movements

There are many neurological studies suggesting that we move our eyes in different directions in a systematic way depending on how we are thinking. You may well have noticed the eye movements people make · as they think and wondered what they mean. Movements of the eyes both up and across seem to be associated with different ways of thinking.

When we look up to the left or right, or defocus the eyes and stare into the distance, this links with thinking in pictures. Have you ever heard someone say, 'Let me *see*,' and seen him stare upwards? Well, seeing is exactly what he is doing, trying to make a picture out of the information you have given him. You may have had the experience of someone 'staring right through you' when you are talking to him. He is thinking about what you are saying by visualising.

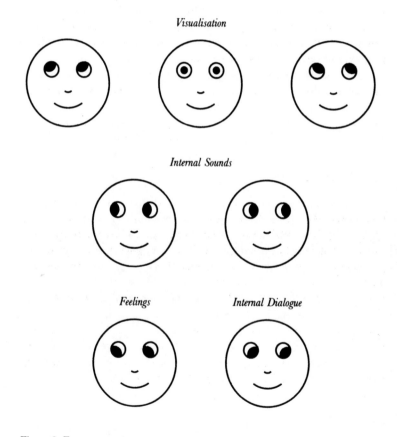

Visualisation

Internal Sounds

Feelings   *Internal Dialogue*

Figure 9 Eye movements

Eye movements across to the right or left show thinking in sounds. Looking down to the left is associated with internal dialogue, talking to yourself.

Looking down to the right accesses feelings; people who are deep in emotional states tend to look down.

These movements are true for the large majority of people, although there are variations. Some people, for example, most of whom will be left-handed, will look down to their left for feelings and down to their right for internal dialogue.

You do not have to take our word for this. Notice how people move their eyes when they think and what words they use as they do so. These eye movements are fascinating because they show *how* people are thinking. They do not, of course, tell you *what* they are thinking.

Unless you pay attention you will miss these subtle clues, so be alert. Whenever you ask a question, there will *always* be an eye movement shift. Watch for it as well as paying attention to what the customer says. Questions demand thought; you cannot not respond to a question, that is their power.

When you do notice the eye movements, how can you use them?

- Suppose the customer says something like, 'I am not really sure, I need something else.' As she does so, she looks up (a visual eye movement).

    You can be very exact in your reply. 'What can I *show* you that would help?' You are tailoring your words to the eye movement.
- When a customer shows by his eye movements that he is thinking, *stop talking*. Do it naturally, not abruptly, and give him a chance to think about what you have said. If you continue to talk, he will not hear you anyway. He is inside his own head.

The eye movement will also tell you the final step in the customer's decision. This is usually one of four possibilities:

- It looks right.
- It feels right.
- It sounds right.
- It makes sense.

A visual eye movement will tell you that for a final buying decision, it must *look* right. The customer has to build a picture of what the product is and how it will solve the problem. The picture may be of himself or others using the product successfully, not of the product itself.

Ask, 'How can I help you to build a picture that looks right to you?'

Eye movements that go down to the left show internal dialogue and probably mean that the final step is that it has to *make sense*. This is where logical arguments may prevail. Current research indicates that only about 10 per cent of the population decide by this means; the largest group (about 40 per cent) buy when it looks right.

Sometimes customers will give you a longer strategy in answer to your question.

For example, 'Well, I would like to *see* some literature, then *talk* to some previous customers before I can *feel* this product is for me.' This is very helpful. It gives three steps and tells you exactly what you have to do to make it easy for the customer to decide.

The principle in these examples is to pay attention to the customer and take what she says literally. Customers will actually tell you exactly how to sell to them if you listen carefully. So often we miss out because we have decided in advance what we think will work or apply some selling technique regardless.

VALUES AND DECISION

Key Points

- A need consists of a present problem and a better future. Develop both in the customer and the client organisation.
- Use questions to move up from a specific solution to the general need.
- Use questions to move down from a general need to a specific solution.
- *Values* are what is important. They are often emotional states we move *towards* or *away from*.
- *Criteria* are values applied in a particular context.
- *Criterial equivalents* are what has to happen for those criteria to be fulfilled.
- Competitors are alternative solutions to the problem that you are not offering.
- Decision strategies are how the customer decides to buy. You can often see them in the customer's eye movements.

- The final step will be:
    It looks right.
    It feels right.
    It sounds right.
    It makes sense.

9

PRESENTATIONS

Presentations to groups, such as partnerships and purchasing committees, can be daunting, especially if there is a big order at stake and a large group of people are waiting for you to impress them. However, the principles of good presentations are the same whether you have a big audience or just one person in front of you.

There are three aspects to a good presentation:

- a good emotional state
- thorough preparation
- good presentation skills

EMOTIONAL STATE

Imagine you are having a really bad day. Nothing has worked out. You feel down. Then a friend calls from home. 'Hey,' he says, 'I've just signed for a big parcel for you, are you expecting any bulky presents?'

You feel much better. It is your birthday in a couple of weeks. Could it be an early present from your relatives in America? Perhaps it is the books you ordered at long last? Or that competition you entered...?

You suddenly feel on top of the world. You decide to finish the calls you have scheduled and go out to celebrate. Suddenly work starts to go well. Feeling wonderful, you go home. However, when you unwrap the parcel, which was not as large as your imagination had made it, it turns out to be some home furnishings. Nice, but not what you hoped for. Yet your expectations had made a difference to your day.

It does not matter how you get into a good emotional state, the results are the same. What happens in the outside world affects us emotionally and our emotional states in turn shape the results we get in the world.

To manage your emotional state, use the exercises in the self-management section of this book, especially the resource anchoring, which involves setting a trigger to get you into a good state (see pp.157–9).

Arrive early for presentations and while you relax for a few moments, mentally rehearse how you want it to go. Feelings of 'nerves' are quite normal. All actors, musicians and performers experience them. 'Nerves' is sometimes another label for 'excitement'.

If you find you are nervous and you want to become calmer, relax your neck and jaw muscles and exhale deeply. The myth of the 'good deep breath' is only half right. You need to exhale deeply to prevent the build up of carbon dioxide in the bloodstream, one of the physiological causes of anxiety. Changing your breathing is probably the most powerful way you can change your state.

This links in with how our emotional state is expressed in our physiology. Try this experiment:

> Put this book down and stand up. Now look down at the book, round and sag your shoulders. Allow your knees to slacken and your posture to droop. Now, without changing your posture, feel confident and determined.
>
> Now hold the book and stand up straight. Stretch your shoulders and breathe in and out deeply and completely. Stand square on your feet and balance your weight evenly. Hold your chin up and look straight ahead. Now, without moving, feel hesitant and uncertain.

You probably found it impossible to experience a feeling inside that was not compatible with your body language. Your physiology is both a product of and a cause of your state. Acting as if you are confident makes you feel more confident.

What goes on inside our heads and hearts influences our body and how we feel. It also influences what we are capable of doing. You won't climb a mountain if you don't think you can.

THOROUGH PREPARATION

Always know the outcome you want from a presentation. It may be a sale, but it need not be. There are other possibilities. It may be to get past this group to a higher level of management or to allocate budget.

Ask yourself some questions to clarify your outcome before the presentation:

- 'What is my key objective?'
- 'What basic message am I putting across?' Summarise it in one sentence.
- 'What are likely to be the main obstacles to this objective?'
- 'What are the benefits to the company?'
- 'Are there any natural allies or potential opposition in the group I am presenting to?'
- 'Do I have all the facts I need for this presentation?'
- 'Do I need a secondary proposal if the first is turned down?'
- 'Are there any special events around the timing of the presentation that can help me or hinder me?'
- 'What is the most difficult question that I could be asked?'

Know what flexibility you have in terms of price, costs, times and extras.

Know the names and positions of the people at the presentation, especially the key decision-makers.

GOOD PRESENTATION SKILLS

Your presentation skills give your words life. It is not a good idea to use a 'canned' presentation. Why not? What is the intention of completely composing a presentation in advance? It is to allay your feelings of nerves. Rehearse, prepare and practise, certainly, but subordinate the material to your individuality and the unique situation. You want a certain outcome. If you fix your presentation too rigidly, then instead of being a means to an end, it becomes an end in itself. You may or may not get your outcome. By building in flexibility you can notice how the presentation is going and change if necessary to keep on track. Leadership, as the saying goes, is the ability to change the second half of the sentence depending on the reaction you get to the first half. Have you ever heard a colleague say, 'I gave a really excellent presentation, but they still didn't buy. What's the matter with them?' Excellent perhaps, but excellent according to whom?

Be yourself in the presentation. This is easy to say and not so easy to do. Yet your sense of self and congruence are more important than all the presentation skills you could learn, useful as these are. Congruence and a sense of self are products of knowing your values and your purpose, and we will deal with this in detail in the self-management section (see p.131).

In fact, presentation skills are very simple. There are a number of things to do and a number of things to avoid.

Beginning the presentation

The first few seconds of a presentation set the audience's expectations. Think of a musical concert: a few wrong notes in the body of a piece will not be remarked on, but they are very noticeable right at the beginning.

Make your first outcome to gain rapport with the audience. This is very simple: get them to share some experience as a group. Humour works well – and make it natural. If you are going to tell a joke, make sure it is a good one. A group that starts by laughing together is the best possible group. Otherwise, refer to some shared experience – the journey, the weather, it does not matter what.

Secondly, establish your credibility. Introduce yourself briefly, say who invited you to present or give any other appropriate referrals. You are reminding the audience (and perhaps yourself) that you are an invited guest.

Thirdly, establish a mood of acceptance right from the start. You can do this with quite mundane remarks or with rhetorical questions. 'We are all here, aren't we?' 'The projector is plugged in, isn't it?' 'Can we open a window – it's a bit stuffy in here, isn't it?'

Don't underestimate the power of the obvious. That's why it *is* obvious, because it is powerful.

Fourthly, set out the way you plan the presentation right from the start. There is a lot of truth in the saying, 'Tell them what you are going to tell them. Tell them, then tell them what you have told them.'

Make *KISS* your motto: **K**eep **I**t **S**hort and **S**imple. More sales are lost through overselling than underselling. The more points you make, the more there is to argue with. Very few people *remember* more than five points from a presentation anyway. Decide in advance which five you want them to remember. People have the greatest recall of what was said in the first few minutes and the last few minutes, so make the key points there.

Mix the sense words that you use: use feeling, seeing and hearing predicates equally, to engage the attention of all the people present. Show them visually with diagrams, pictures and slides, tell them loud and clear and make the experience real for them.

Also, use associations to emphasise the important points of your presentation. Make the same gesture every time you make the same important point. This emphasises the point non-verbally.

Be aware of your audience

Have some notes on your presentation and refer to them if you need to, otherwise stay in contact with your audience. You will know which points are well received and which are not by watching and listening to your audience. You cannot do this if you are looking down, reading.

When you see a positive response, emphasise the point. When you see a negative response, slide over it. When you see furrowed brows or quizzical expressions, say it again a different way or go into explanatory detail. *What is important is not so much what you say, but your audience's reaction to it.* Think of them and think about getting the reaction you want.

Eye contact

Eye contact is a natural expression of your interest. The more you show you are interested in your audience, the more they will be interested in what you have to say.

Make eye contact with everyone in the room before beginning your presentation and continue to make eye contact with different people as you speak. Let your eyes describe a figure of eight across the room.

Eye contact for about five seconds works best. Resist the temptation to dart your eyes away immediately you make contact. A prolonged stare is not very successful either.

Posture

The way you hold your body makes a fundamental statement about who you are and, as we have seen, posture strongly affects how we think. Stand erect if you are standing to make your presentation or sit comfortably with your back straight. Avoid distracting swaying movements.

To find out your good basic standing posture, stand with your back to a wall. Touch the wall with the back of your head, your backside and as much of the small of your back as you comfortably can. Check with friends and in a mirror that what feels right is not actually leaning to the right or left. Sometimes we get used to postures which feel right, even though looking from the outside they are unbalanced.

Be spontaneous!

Impossible, unfortunately. The moment you *try* to be spontaneous, you cannot. And yet good presentations have that spontaneous, easy quality about them. The answer is to stop doing those things that prevent you being natural. Look for nervous gestures to eliminate – jangling coins in your pocket, picking your fingers, shifting from side to side, brushing your hair back, etc. Also avoid unnecessary gestures. Let gestures come naturally (or not) from the presentation you are giving.

Let your voice add energy and interest to the presentation. Good material will sink like lead if delivered in a monotone, so let your voice be expressive. The normal speaking rate is about 150 words a minute. If you speak considerably more slowly than this, you will risk a drop in the energy levels of both yourself and your audience. For many people, speed of speech equals enthusiasm and energy. However, if people are taking notes, slow down to a level where you can see they are comfortable.

You do not have to speak at 150 words a minute *all the time*. Use pauses as a natural punctuation for what you say. This gives both you and the audience a chance to collect your thoughts.

How you breathe affects your voice and your whole physiology; breathe deeply and remember to breathe out! Nervous breathing is quick and shallow; it deprives your voice of power and increases the nervous feelings by increasing the amount of carbon dioxide in the blood.

If your work involves many important presentations, practise speaking into a tape recorder and playing yourself back. It will be an ear-opener. We never hear ourselves as others hear us because our voice resonates in the bones in our skull. Then ask, is the voice you hear on the tape recorder the one you want your audience to hear?

What to avoid

- *Overuse of the passive tense.*
  The passive tense is reactive, for example, 'The presentation was given by me.' The active tense is proactive, for example, 'I gave the presentation.' Things are made ponderous by the passive tense, are they not?

- *Rambling.*
  Sentences in the form of 'It is because ... that...' are difficult to follow.

Long sentences are also hard to follow. People tend to lose track of a sentence after about 15 words.

- *Ums and ahs.*
  You may have a personal nervous word or phrase. 'Ummmm ... ah... You know what I mean ... OK....?' (Sniff.) Er ... cut the verbal fluff, beginning with the most frequent.

- *Clichés and current business jargon.*
  At the end of the day, buzz words may alienate the man in the street. When push comes to shove, if you hit the ground running with ongoing situations, the silent majority will hear verbal papering over cracks. If you use new terms, make sure you are using them for a specific reason and not just to impress or to sound like everyone else. To attempt to match in this way may have the opposite result than the one you seek.

Questions

People at the presentation are sure to ask questions. This is good, it can remind you of an important point or you can utilise it to mention another feature of the product as you answer. Never be afraid to say you do not know (but will find out). Difficult questions need only be difficult once.

Whatever happens in the presentation, learn from it afterwards. When you did well, congratulate yourself and ask, 'How might I have done better?' When it did not go as planned, ask, 'What must I do different next time to make sure that does not happen again?'

Give yourself permission to make mistakes; the best in every field do – but only once.

Negotiation

You may have to negotiate in a presentation. Negotiation is not about confrontation, it is about achieving a shared outcome: win–win. It is the process of getting what you want from others by giving them what they want. In negotiation, differences are brought out into the open, where they are much less dangerous. The shared solution must work in practice. Any point that is too frail to stand up to discussion before the contract is signed is sure to cause trouble afterwards. The clearer you are in negotiation the more you protect yourself and generate trust.

Set your limits before you start. The first rule of negotiation is not to negotiate with yourself in front of others. Be clear what you can give away and what you want in return. Think about which concessions will have the most impact on the customer. It will not necessarily be price. Be guided by the customer's decision criteria. Do not start too low or you will have nowhere else to go. If you use up all your concession in one go, you will have nothing left, especially if a competitor matches your concession. Start near the top of your range and make concessions by small increments, slower and slower and more and more unwillingly.

Use questions. They give you thinking time and are a good alternative to disagreement. Use backtracking (see p.77) and test for agreement as you go. If misunderstandings persist, an angry customer may end up feeling cheated.

Separate understanding from agreement. You can show by backtracking that you understand the customer's position without agreeing with it. When the customer puts forward a proposal, do not put forward a counter-proposal immediately, for this is the time when he is least interested in your offering. Discuss his proposal first. Ask him about it and put yours forward after that.

Negotiation is not selling. It is one aspect of selling, starting from differences to reach agreement. Your skill in negotiation can make a difference in a major sale.

PRESENTATIONS

Key Points

- There are three aspects to a good presentation:
    a good emotional state
    thorough preparation
    good presentation skills
- Be clear on what you want to achieve from the presentation.
- Use good presentation skills:
    Your audience's reaction to what you say is more important than your expressed intention.
    Be natural.
    Make your presentation multi-sensory.
- Do not negotiate unless you have to (negotiation is the process of getting what you want from others by giving them what they want).

10

CLOSING AND CUSTOMER SERVICE

CLOSING

In the Old Bazaar, the close was the focal point of the sale. It was where everything had been leading. It was make or break time. In the Old Bazaar, when you were about to close, imaginary crowds gathered to watch, trumpeters played a fanfare, you placed all your eggs in one basket, took a deep breath and asked for the order.

Here are some Old Bazaar examples (slightly exaggerated):

- The Authority Close – 'Go on, BUY IT!'
- The Guilt Close: 'I have put such a lot of effort and time into this, you owe it to me to buy.'
- The Hypnotic Close – 'Can you not feel an urge to BUY NOW you know this product is for you, wasn't it?'
- The Economy Close – 'Think how much money you will save on this special offer. You can't afford *not* to buy.' (Countered by: 'If I have no need for the product, I can save even more money by not buying at all!')
- The Guillotine Close – 'I am afraid I can only offer this price today. Tomorrow prices have to rise by 30 per cent.'
- The Confusion Close – 'I can see you are the kind of adventurous person who likes the challenge of buying something you have doubts about.'
- The Scarcity Close – 'This is the last one I have. I am not sure when we will be getting them again.'

Such manipulative closes have had their day. In the New Bazaar, the close is a choice and the natural result of all that has gone before. It is a choice both you and the customer make. Do you, the salesperson, want this person as a customer? And does the customer want you, your company and product? If there is not a positive response to this choice from *both* elements of the buying/selling process, the close will not happen.

To reach this choice point you will need to be certain of three things:

- That the customer is qualified.
- That the product meets his need and his criteria, from his viewpoint.
- That the sale is a winning move for both of you.

Timing

When and if you close, timing is all important. Someone's internal state, how he feels inside, what he is thinking, manifests itself in his external or visible behaviour. That's how you know when someone close to you is feeling different inside, because his external behaviour – posture, colouring, movements, mannerisms – change. It's the recognition of these changes in external behaviour that prompts you to ask, 'What's up?' because you want to know what has changed in his internal state to create this change in his external behaviour. This change may be a signal that he needs your help or support, or that he is feeling really good inside.

With friends and relations you may find it easy to read their external behaviour and know what internal state it represents because you know them well. With people who are new to you, even if you have had a number of meetings with them, your natural, unconscious ability to absorb and understand the signs will not be so refined.

In the Old Bazaar, external behaviour is generalised and made applicable to all. In the New Bazaar, we say everyone is different. You need to read the non-verbal, external behaviour of the individual in order to be certain you are reading the internal state of the individual. This is *calibrating*. You need to talk with the customer about something pleasant to him in order to read or calibrate his non-verbal messages that go with feeling good. You need to talk about uncertainties in the past to be able to read or calibrate all the signs that go with uncertainty. Do both of these things early in the interview as part of the small talk. Take a mental snapshot of both states. It is only by reading individuals in this way that you will be able to time your close to suit you and the customer. Do not close when you calibrate uncertainty.

A well timed close is always successful.

Encountering a lot of objections tells you that your close was premature.

Closing the sale is very simple. You have to ask for the order. Do not introduce new information, it will simply be confusing. Backtrack the discussion, linking product to need and criteria. Once you have asked, be quiet and wait. You will be able to tell what the customer's answer will be by reading his external behaviour.

How you ask for the order is also important – not so much the words you use as the way you use them. Your words must communicate that you are certain your proposal is right for the customer and, more importantly, your non-verbal messages must say the same thing. With so much of our communication being non-verbal, if there is a clash between our verbal and non-verbal messages, an incongruence, it will be the non-verbal message that will register as being the truth. If you look hesitant when asking, 'Is it all right to go ahead then?' you will trigger doubt in the customer's mind. In order to avoid this incongruence you need to do two things:

- Be absolutely clear that your proposal is right for the customer and that you have created a win–win relationship.
- Know that selling is an act of giving and not an act of taking away.

When product meets need and criteria, you will not need any special closing techniques.

Dealing with questions and objections

Questions and objections help you clarify the customer's need. They point to customer's criteria either directly or indirectly. During the course of a meeting or a series of meetings, customers are bound to ask you questions and raise issues or objections. At first these might throw you off course. You might feel like a sailor making good headway suddenly hit by a sideways wind. You have a choice: either you fight the wind or pretend it is not there or try to harness the power it can give you. The choice you make will be influenced by your interpretation of the customer's intention. If you choose to believe that the question, issue or objection is thrown into the conversation to cause trouble or halt proceedings, then it is likely you will resist. If you interpret the customer's intention as being positive, to seek more information, greater understanding and clarification, then you will harness the wind and make faster progress towards your destination.

Questions

Answer customer questions as far as you are able, except when:

- The question is a technical one. Although you may have an answer, it is usually best referred to your technical backup. Precision questions about features and how they work fall into this category.
- The customer knows the answer already. Why is he asking? Not to find out the answer to that question. Stay away from guessing games.
- You cannot commit yourself or your company to what the customer wants. Negotiate rather than answer.
- You do not know. Just say so. Offer to find out and give the customer the answer later.

Objections

An objection is always valid for the customer. To address it, you have to look at it from her point of view. If she states an objection, turn it into a question. Say something like, 'I understand you are concerned about ... [backtrack what she said]. Is there a particular question you have about that aspect...?'

It's like the vending machine salesman who thought he had defined the need and criteria of a customer to his complete satisfaction, only to be hit at the last moment by the statement, 'We've done a survey. The staff don't want to drink the rubbish you get from those machines.' All of the efficiency, savings and hygiene benefits had been suddenly swept aside.

Able to maintain his state and rapport, but only just, as he saw his hard-earned commission go flying out of the window, the salesperson asked what question the customer really wanted to ask. After much support and encouragement, the customer said, 'What will happen if the quality of the drinks deteriorates and the staff complain? What will management think of my decision then?' Having reached that point, a guarantee on quality control was all that was needed to re-establish the sale.

Objections and issues usually come down to one of the following messages:

- *I need more time to make a decision.*
  Give the time and set up another meeting or contact to review progress. Never leave it open-ended. It may be that a manager needs to evaluate all the bids she has received and then make a

decision. It may be that there are criteria still to be addressed. Watch the customer and ask, 'What do you still need to know?' or 'What area are you still uncertain about?'

Often another person needs to be involved in the decision. If appropriate, ask if you can be there too. You are the best advocate for your own product. A customer may simply need to get several viewpoints from different, perhaps neutral, people before coming to a decision, in which case make that as easy as possible. He may also want names of previous clients he can talk to.

- *Thank you. I want to shop around.*
  Say, 'Naturally, it is absolutely right to explore the market before committing yourself. Do you have any questions I can answer right now?'

  You could also ask, 'Who else will you be talking to?' or 'Who else will you be seeing?'

- *I do not like some parts of the product.*
  Ask, 'Which parts exactly are you unhappy about?' It would be a pity if an all or nothing decision (buy or not buy) hinged on a part that might be changeable or negotiable.

- *Money.*
  There are two possible objections here:

  It's too cheap.
  This may mean the customer does not trust you and she is saying, 'Where's the catch?' Low price equals poor quality in her mind. This is a credibility issue. You need to show your customer that whatever the price, your product meets her criteria. If your price is seriously below the general market price, this can paradoxically be a drawback. You must explain why it is so low.

  It's too expensive.
  The budget may not be available. Ask, 'If we can find a way to deal with the price issue that satisfies you, would you buy?' If the customer says 'Yes', then negotiate round price. Beware of setting up a lose—win situation where you reduce your price just to make the sale. It is usually unrealistic and sets the buyer up to lose later. Always tell buyers they are getting a special deal, when you are prepared to offer one. Make it completely specific to the one sale and make it clear that there are no strings attached. The customer does not want to buy a debt as well as a product.

  If you ask 'If we can find a way to deal with the price issue, would you buy?' and the customer says 'No' or hesitates, then there are either other objections or the money issue is not negotiable.

It is usually better not to negotiate on price if you can possibly help it. Value for money often hides behind the price objection. If money was unlimited we could buy anything and everything we wanted. Alas, it is not. Money represents scarcity and choice. Spending money on one thing means we cannot have something else. Money is a measure of value. We decide where to spend money based on our value hierarchy.

Customers will pay more for added value, usually one of the three 'R's:

Reputation
Reliability
Relationship

There are two further ways to deal with the price objection. They both involve cost analysis.

The first is a cost-effectiveness comparison. Given the customer's need, your product is the most cost-effective way of meeting it. This argument hinges on the away from element of the customer's need. He *must* do something, the only question is, what?

The second is a cost benefit analysis. You show that the measurable benefits of having the product are greater than the cost. This aspect is based on the towards aspect of the need – future benefit.

If you believe that there is an unvoiced block to progress and you are not sure what the real objection is, there are a number of questions that help surface objections. The most general one is:

'Is there anything that prevents you making a decision about this today?'

In cases where the customer simply seems uncertain, you may need to fish for the specific objection to help crystallise it. Useful questions are:

'Are you satisfied about the cost and the financing options?'
'Are you satisfied with the guarantee and the service?'
'Is there something I did not fully explain to you?'
'Is it the right price/timing/length...?'

'What is the main concern you have left?'

As you deal with objections, you can find out about others that still need attention by using what is called the *conditional close.*' The general form of the conditional close is, '*If* this and this were to happen, *then* would you buy?'

Ask, 'If this issue were resolved to your satisfaction, would there be anything else that would need to be addressed?

This is a powerful question, so take care – it may be received as harassment if you ask it persistently.

There is an interesting pattern of behaviour that you have probably met called the *polarity response* or Devil's Advocate. People who use this pattern of behaviour will find some point to disagree on whatever you say. Their favourite phrase is 'Yes, but...' This can be annoying and really all they are doing is looking for the exception. They are addicted to looking for difference. Polarity responders are easy to deal with because they are so consistent. Simply phrase in the negative. Instead of saying, 'You will like this,' say, 'I'm not sure whether you will like this.' Do not say, 'This will interest you,' say, 'This may not interest you.' For those readers who are polarity responders, this paragraph may not be quite what you were looking for...

Dealing with criticism, anger and insults

Sometimes customer objections mean 'Go away', but indirectly. In order of importance, under fire, you need to:

- Keep a resourceful state.
- Respond and do something if the customer has a legitimate grievance.
- Extract any useful learning for yourself and your company.

Staying resourceful

The first principle in dealing with abuse or anger is to look at it objectively. Anger and criticism are hard to take directly. Instead, imagine stepping outside yourself and seeing yourself taking the criticism. Detaching yourself in this way allows you to think clearly and stops any bad feelings. There is no longer anyone 'at home'. This is called *dissociation.* From this detached position you can evaluate the criticism objectively.

Another way you can protect yourself is to imagine a clear plastic screen between you and the other person. Watch the vitriol bounce off the screen.

From this safe position, separate the information the angry customer is giving you from the way he is giving it. Now you have a choice of what to do:

- You might want to agree with him (with what he is saying, not how he is saying it).
- You may want to apologise, for yourself and/or on your company's behalf.
- You may want to leave the issue for the moment, because you need more information from another source.
- You may want to give your version of events, or disagree with the customer completely and let him know that. Don't get heated yourself. Insults in cold blood are unacceptable. Walk away or respond wittily as you prefer.

The customer may contact you and apologise, then you both can rebuild the relationship (if you wish).

Defusing the situation

When you respond, match slightly *under* the volume and intensity of the customer's voice tone. Acknowledge her legitimate concern and gradually lead her down to a more reasoned state. *Then* use your words to defuse the situation, in the way already outlined in 'telephone skills':

1. First, acknowledge the comment. This paces the customer.
2. Secondly, ask for information about what needs to be different.
3. Thirdly, backtrack and use the conditional close.

For example:

Customer: 'Your delivery was late last week, I wasted a whole afternoon!'

Salesperson (voice matching the urgent tone): 'No wonder you are upset! What can I do now to help?' (Acknowledgment.)

Customer: 'Don't tell me a delivery is coming when it isn't!'

Salesperson: 'We do not do that deliberately, I can assure you. First I'll find out what happened at our end. What can we do to make sure this does not happen again?' (Ask for information.)

Customer: 'Telephone when it leaves the warehouse!'

Salesperson: 'If I let you know what happened and see if it is feasible to telephone when the next consignment leaves, is that enough?' (Conditional close.)

The main quality of this approach is that you do not agree to anything; you find out what has to happen for the customer to be satisfied. You may or may not be able to meet his demands completely, but the immediate situation is defused.

CUSTOMER SERVICE

Customer service is a vast area and we will only touch on it here. Nearly all companies accept the value of customer service. Yet many still do not live up to their own expectations. 'Customer Care' and 'Putting the Customer First' are philosophies that are widely proffered but not so widely adhered to.

When you have confirmed business, it is more effective to view the sale as the beginning of your next sale rather that the end of the current one. It will then be like a door opening rather than one shutting. Set up another meeting to discuss future needs. If there is a contract to be signed, have two copies and both sign. This gives you both equality. Lastly, send a personal letter of thanks to the customer within a day and do not have a secretary sign it in your stead.

Long-term planning is the ability to project present decisions into the future. Describe your procedure for the delivery or implementation of the purchase and how your company would handle any problems. Make sure the customer has a contact and knows what to do in the event of a problem. A long-term relationship with a customer is built on trust, not that nothing will go wrong, but that when it does you can put it right. The long-term relationship is more important than any short-term problem.

Ask your customer his criteria for resolving a problem. Should a problem arise, what sort of response would be satisfactory? Do the downside planning now, while the relationship is good and you are together. 'They all lived happily ever after' only happens in fairy tales.

Many companies will not allow their salespeople to be involved in any aspect of implementation or follow up of an order. They want their salespeople out there selling. The intention behind this approach is understandable. Salespeople are expensive. Cheaper people can deal with the customer once the order is signed.

However, this type of thinking ignores the impact on future business of customer satisfaction. It needs only one aspect of delivery or use to go wrong for that customer to stop being a source of positive referrals and become a bearer of bad news. Also, some customers need constant reassurance that they have made the right decision. Therefore, it is important to keep contact with customers. A phone call will do. If and when something goes wrong, you will want to give the customer your attention and sort out the problem. Do not ignore the 98 per cent of the time when things go right. Imagine a new buyer was looking through a file of your relationship with the customer. Write a letter when times are good, saying how glad you are that all is well and offering your further help if needed. Keep a strong relationship with your client companies.

Part of building the relationship is not just protecting and maintaining the account but developing it as well. There is a good deal of research that indicates that accounts are lost to the active salespeople of competitive companies, unless you develop the relationship. A good customer is also an excellent reference site. Your relationship is never static. If it is not developing then it is declining. Resting on your laurels is not enough. The question to ask your customer is, 'How *else* can I be of service to you?'

When checking up on your own support people, do not behave like a policeman suspecting failure. If failure is what you suspect, it is likely to be what you get. When asking people to report back on progress, do not ask only for bad news. 'If anything goes wrong, let me know.' It is an exceptional person who rushes to report back that they've got something wrong. Rather, 'Let me know when it's all in and working.'

There are two simple rules to ensuring good customer service:

• Treat your customer in the way that you would need to be treated in order that you would continue to use a supplier. (Second position the customer by putting yourself into his position.)
• Do what you say you're going to do. Dependability is highly valued

because, unfortunately, it is in short supply.

Do these consistently and you will build a reputation. Such a reputation is priceless. It generates customers, referrals and gives you an edge over your competitors.

CLOSING AND CUSTOMER SERVICE

Key Points

CLOSING
- Closing is a choice not a requirement.
- Calibrate the customer and read non-verbal signals to know when to close.
- Close congruently.
- Dealing with objections:
    Objections are always valid – turn them into specific questions.
    Surface objections and use the conditional close.
    Deal with the price objection by:
      added value
      cost-effectiveness comparison
      cost benefit analysis
- Dealing with criticism:
    Keep a resourceful state. Dissociate and evaluate the criticism.
    Act if the customer has a legitimate grievance.
    Extract any useful learning for yourself and your company.
    Defuse the situation by pacing and leading voice tone:
      acknowledge the concern
      seek information
      backtrack and conditional close

CUSTOMER SERVICE
- A completed sale is a beginning of the next phase – customer care.
- Take second position by thinking of yourself as the customer.
- Do what you say you're going to do.

PART THREE

LOOKING AFTER YOURSELF

11

CONGRUENCE

The first part of this book redefines the cultural attitude to sales and how this affects salespeople and customers. The second part covers the skills of a successful salesperson in the New Bazaar. This third part is about finding your sense of self and taking care of yourself. In this section, you are the customer and selling is the product. Is it for you?

We have no vested interest in you 'buying' selling. We simply wish to explore whether or not selling is the solution to your need. This section is about you – what you want, what is important to you, how you work and how your work fits into your life and your identity. Why do we cover these areas? Surely, everybody has to work, so just get on with it. No. We cover self-management because no matter what work you do, your sense of self and your personal happiness come first. If you do not have a good relationship with yourself and your work, no amount of skills training will compensate.

We want to support you in what you want to do. This book may, however, reinforce the thought that selling is not for you. This is fine. You cannot be judged a failure at something you do not want to do. This book is written to enable you to be as good as you want to be. Your personal values determine your peak of performance. Otherwise you risk treating yourself like a customer who is manipulated into buying something, not from his own need, but from the need and values of others.

There is a mythical story about a man named Procrustes. Procrustes owned a house passed by many travellers. He was very hospitable and had a guest room which contained an enormous and extremely comfortable bed. Travellers were invited to stay the night and sleep in the bed. There was, as you might imagine, a price to be paid. A traveller who was too short for the bed was stretched on the rack until he was long enough. If the traveller was too tall for the bed, Procrustes would cut enough off his feet to make sure he fitted. A heavy price to pay for a place to stay.

TAKING CARE OF YOURSELF

When recruiting, many sales managers look for salespeople who are in financial difficulties in the belief that such people will sell themselves out of trouble. They see debt, and the threat it carries, as motivation that will relieve them, the managers, of the responsibility of managing the salesperson's performance. 'What we want are really hungry people,' is an often expressed desire, and if they can be hungry for food as well as success, all the better. Other managers look for people who will strive to be the top performer, no matter what sacrifice it takes. Health, family, friends, hobbies and peace of mind are seen as acceptable offerings to the god of winning. When a top performer is burnt out you can always look for another one.

As salespeople, we must be aware that business is such that most companies value our results above ourselves. 'You're only as good as last month's figures,' echoes around most sales offices. In sales, 'more' generally equals 'better'. Bigger volume means more success. But you are free to define – or redefine – what being a success means to you. By drawing boundaries around what we are prepared to pay for what we receive we are not short changing the company that pays us. We are simply establishing a balance that will allow us to perform to an effective and efficient level over a long period of time without losing our health and happiness in the process.

Try a small experiment before going further. Without thinking at length, complete the following sentence:

Selling is like...

Did the answer surprise you? If selling is like that, what does that make you?

Another question. Again, just take the first thing that comes into your head.

I would like selling to be like...
Then I would be...

Congruence

Congruence is that state of alignment when you believe in what you are doing and your body and mind are working towards your goal. Personal congruence and a sense of self come as by-products of knowing what you want and what is important to you. Congruence itself has a 'buy-product' – it is your greatest quality as a salesperson. Customers sense it and will buy into it by buying from you.

How congruent you are shows in your body language. Your body language in turn affects the thoughts and feelings that make up your internal state.

For example, someone is asked to speak in front of a group. If the message in her head and heart is negative – 'I don't want to do this, the group looks hostile, if I mess up I won't get the business, if I don't get the business then I might lose my job, etc.' – these negative feelings may bring about an external state of drooped shoulders, sagging knees, side on glances, croaking voice, etc. This negative physiology then returns the message to the internal state, reinforcing it. This reinforced negative internal state returns an even worse message. And so it goes on and on. The longer you wait to speak, the worse it gets. Likewise, if you're presenting a product that you believe is overpriced, of poor quality or does not address the customer's need, your own doubt and negative feelings will influence your own external behaviour. Your physiology may shrink, you may find it hard to hold eye contact, your voice quality may change – whatever is your natural response will happen.

We can all read these external messages. We don't have to be trained in body language to know that something is not right. We just know when something does not fit together, and that sense of knowing creates buyer's caution and delays and encourages customers to get a second opinion.

Congruence is the strongest sales force you have and the paradox is, you cannot manufacture it. It arises naturally, or not, from your thoughts, feelings and behaviour.

Balance of life

Our profession is an important part, although only one part, of our lives. We have many parts to our lives and act differently in each. If we have to deal with one of our children, a partner, a colleague, a boss, a customer or an angry motorist, we will access the side of ourselves best suited to the situation. It is as if there is a part of you that likes being at work, another that likes being with the family, another that likes to socialise, another that likes to be alone and so on. We are more like an orchestra of soloists than a single identity. And all of these soloists need their time and place. Parts that are ignored or restricted will find a way of gaining the time and space they need to survive.

One way of doing this is to undermine the attention other parts are receiving. Parts of ourselves are rather like children that you ignore at your peril, for they have many ways to get your attention, and the more you ignore them, the more insistent they become. And they do not play fair. A part that likes to be with the family will grab your attention if you channel all your time and energy into professional duties. It may take hold of your internal voice when you are at work and whisper, 'The kids will call you "uncle" soon.' 'They'll hate you when they're older.' 'Fancy missing a birthday, bad boy.'

When this internal voice gets to work, your internal state will be drawn down by whispers of doubt about the product, the company, your life etc., your external behaviour will start to communicate negative non-verbal signals, the customers will feel awkward, your business levels will drop and your internal voice will grow in strength. Falling performance, therefore, can often be corrected by working less and playing more rather than working harder. A balanced life removes many of the drains on energy and releases it.

Balance is not static and inflexible. When you balance on a wall you have to make tiny adjustments of your weight the whole time. The best way to unbalance and fall is to try to keep yourself stiffly erect and make no adjustments whatsoever.

How can you work towards balance and congruence? Simple, but not easy. Know what you want, why you want it and how you are going to get it. This means looking at your goals and values, and the ways you communicate with yourself and others.

GOALS – WHAT DO YOU WANT?

12

This is one of the most fundamental questions you can ask yourself. Clear goals are the key to managing both your work and your life. Not knowing what you want makes it really hard to get. A long-term study was started at Stanford University in 1952 to track the lives of a selected group of students. Two per cent wrote out their outcomes and goals, and continued to do so. Ten per cent set goals, but did not write them down. The rest neither wrote nor set goals. Twenty years later, the two per cent who kept written outcomes were worth more money than the other 98 per cent put together. (This, for convenience's sake, presupposes the acquisition of money as being a satisfactory form of measurement.)

Goals, or outcomes, or objectives (the three are synonymous), are what you want, not what you should want or what you do not want. Often we strive to achieve goals only to find the cost of achievement is greater than we are prepared to pay. A mid-life crisis is often the result of finding that the ladder you have been climbing for years has been resting against the wrong wall.

Goal-setting is getting what you want. It is not about pushing yourself hard and never being satisfied. Nor is it about unrealistic positive thinking, jumping out of bed in the morning announcing how great you are, how much you are going to earn and how great today is going to be. Within a week the mirror will talk back and say, 'Who are you trying to kid?'

Outcomes in life are positive things to have as long as they provide a sense of well-being and positive emotions. Always question the value of an outcome towards which the route is painful and tiring. If the journey is not as pleasant as the destination, check that your hidden goal is not to create personal dissatisfaction.

How do you know what you want? You make it up according to your values and motives. Below are rules about setting outcomes that make them achievable, realistic and motivating. This is an extended version of the goal-setting process in the organisation section of this book (see pp.39–43) and is more suitable for exploring what you want in your personal life. You can either record the answers by writing them down or by using the software available (see Consultancy section). You can use this process on anything you want, personal and professional. One question you could explore with this process is: What do I want from my profession?

Phrase it in the positive

You do not go shopping with a list of things you do not want to buy. An outcome like 'I do not want to lose this order' is negative. By thinking this way you will constantly focus on losing the order. A tightrope walker does not think 'I must not *fall*', or guess what will happen? In order not to think of something you have to think of it in order to know what to avoid thinking of...

Turn negative outcomes round by asking, *'What do I want instead?'* So:

'I do not want a job where I have to work weekends' becomes *'I want Saturday and Sunday free.'*
'I do not want to put the customer off' becomes *'I want good rapport with the customer.'*

When, where and with whom?

Make your goal as specific as you can. Ask the same questions of yourself that you ask your customers. Employ Kipling's serving men: what, where, when, how and who.

What do you want exactly?
Where do you want it?
When do you want it? What time frame are you talking about? Weeks, months or years?

If possible, put an exact date for achieving the goal. Have short-term outcomes, long-term, career and life-planning outcomes.

Make the outcome as specific as you can so that you can actually imagine yourself having it. The more exactly you can imagine it, the more you will set up filters in your mind to notice the opportunities that present themselves every day if only you were aware of them.

(Have you ever been interested in buying some item of clothing?·
Suddenly you notice that many people are wearing it. They always
were, only now you notice.)

Conditions and consequences

Are there any conditions under which you would not want this goal?
There are some important questions to ask yourself:

What by-products of your present state are worth keeping? How
comfortable are you with the status quo?
What will you have to sacrifice to get what you want? Is it worth it?

You know as a salesperson that everything has its price tag and it need
not be expressed in money. There is bound to be some investment of
time, for a start:

What would be your time commitment?
How much effort would your goal need?
What money investment would it need?
Who else would be affected and how would they feel about it?
  Will pursuing this outcome deprive (or deprave) your family and
friends? How compatible is your goal with the hopes and fears of
the other significant people in your life who support you? It is
unrealistic to expect their support if they are not getting what they
want as well.
What are the other wider consequences of your goal?

Many of these questions will overlap. They are designed to avoid the
predicament so perfectly expressed in the words of a car sticker we saw
in the rear window of a Mercedes: 'I've worked hard to get where I
am... Where am I?'
  These questions are also all designed to check your congruence. Is
your inner orchestra playing in tune? The situation is a bit like a
complex sale to an organisation where several people have to give their
approval. You are that organisation. For the sale to come through, the
users have to be satisfied, the financial director has to sign the order
and senior management have to approve. Make sure no part of you
vetoes or sabotages your outcome. If it does, don't fight back. If you
resist resistance, it persists. Better to reform your outcome or negotiate a compromise. If the part of you that likes to keep fit is resisted

by the part of you that likes cream cakes, maybe a reduced intake of cakes would offer support to a less speedy fitness programme.

Gather your resources

Make a list of the resources you have that will help you. This is nearly always a pleasure to do. We all have many resources we seldom think about. Resources are divided into three main groups:

- *Personal qualities.*
  List your skills and qualities, such as intelligence, perseverance, leadership and skill at rapport. Do not confine your thoughts to one particular outcome, think what qualities you show in other areas of your life. A woman we know is brilliant at negotiating between her two children when they fight. At work, she does not think she has any 'business' negotiation skills, yet the same skills are needed.

- *People.*
  Many people may be able to help you, both directly and indirectly. Go through your phone book and ask how each person might be a resource. Also, think of people as role models. If Jim is really good at landing big accounts, get curious and find out how he does it. Informally you will be doing what NLP does formally – discovering how excellent people get their results.

- *Things.*
  Obvious examples are money, books, computers and cars.

Evidence

How will you know that you have achieved your goal? You can spend your life looking for something that you have already, like someone looking for the glasses on the end of his nose. Exactly what will you see? What will you hear? What will you feel? For example, if your outcome was to sell into a large corporate account then your evidence might be to see the order, to hear the customer tell you that she is placing the order and to feel the closing handshake, followed by a feeling of pride and achievement.

What will others see, hear and feel? For example, your customer will see you make a final presentation, hear you talk about the product and ask for the order. She will feel confident and comfortable about placing the order with you.

Finally, in all these things, what is the very last piece of evidence before you get the outcome?

Responsibility

Whatever you have set yourself, it is *your* goal and you will have to act to get it. The rest of the world is not going to let it fall in your lap. If you do not know what you want there are many people who will be happy to decide for you. When your goal is out of your control it is just a pie in the sky. Be practical:

What do you have to do?
What do others have to do?

For example, you have a goal to get the Bloggs account. Your sales manager is the person who will decide who gets it. You need to start thinking, 'What can I do to influence the manager to give me this account?' Apart from directly asking, you might familiarise yourself with it and bring to his notice similar accounts where you did well. However deserving you are, don't wait around for others. Be pro-active.

You need to make an action plan. Part of this action plan involves breaking the goal down into smaller steps, exactly as you would in your business goals, as we described in the organisation section (see p.41). The larger the goal, the more it will need to be broken down.

Ask the question, 'What prevents me from achieving this goal?' This starts the process of finding the obstacles that are in your way, so you can set intermediate outcomes towards resolving them. Invariably these obstacles are phrased in the negative. To progress your outcome, rephrase them in the positive by asking the question, 'What do I want *instead*?'

For example, 'What stops me taking exercise?' 'I haven't the time.' 'What do I want instead?' 'I want to create time to exercise.'

At the same time, look in the other direction and notice how your outcome can be a smaller chunk of a larger goal. Ask the question, 'When I have that, what will that give me?'

For example, you want to achieve a high commission this month, say £5,000. There is a deal that is just coming to fruition. What are the obstacles? You need to close with the customer. This may involve making a number of telephone calls and fixing a meeting. The telephone calls, while not very motivating in themselves, gain power by being connected to the larger outcome – they are steps towards earning £5,000. A telephone call equals a move to achieving a high commission. This is a good reason for making the call.

Final check

Last of all, imagine you have that outcome. Does it feel right for *you*? This is the final congruence check.

Now mentally rehearse having that goal fully in the future. What will you see? What will you hear? How will you feel? How will your life be different? This is called *future pacing* in NLP. It makes the goal more real and sometimes as you mentally rehearse what will be different you may come across problems or future goals that you had not thought of.

Both disappointment and success require adequate planning. Disappointment is the success of getting what you did not want, because you did not think your goal out well enough beforehand.

ACHIEVING YOUR GOALS: SENSITIVITY AND FLEXIBILITY

Once you know what you want, be sensitive to what you are getting. You may know where you want to be, but if you do not know where you are now, it's hard to move forward. Journeys do not always go smoothly. An aeroplane is slightly off course 95 per cent of the time, first in one direction, then in another. However, an aeroplane's instruments are sensitive enough to identify when the plane is off course and help the pilot make corrections. Without these corrections the New York flight could end up in San Francisco (and heaven knows where your luggage would be). Apply this same principle of monitoring progress and correction to your goals.

Once you know where you are going and know where you are now, what choices do you have about what to do? In sales there are no 'right' answers, just more answers, more choices. Use those that work for you. Leave those that do not. When a customer rejects one approach, this becomes a signal to use another. If you want to be *ineffective*, just do more of the same that was not working already. Do it more and harder, like the stereotype of the Englishman in a foreign country. When the people do not understand him, he simply says the same thing more s – l – o – w – l – y and LOUDLY.

Different points of view

As we have already discussed, one part of having a flexible approach is to be able to see the same situation from different points of view. There is your point of view, your reality, what you believe and think is true, called first position. Then there is the other person's point of view, his reality, what he believes and thinks is true. His view is as true for him as your reality is for you. When you appreciate someone else's point of view, NLP calls this second position. Rapport gives you a better sense of second position.

The three basic mistakes in selling all stem from a lack of second position:

1. Not taking the customer's point of view into account.
2. Thinking the customer's point of view is the same as your own.
3. Seeing the customer's point of view, but discarding it as irrelevant or mistaken.

Lastly, there is the detached view that takes into account both parties and how they relate together – third position.

You need to be clear and congruent about your own view. And you need to be able to see the product from the customer's perspective and understand her need. You also need to be able to detach yourself, particularly in stressful situations, and appreciate the direction of the whole conversation.

To mentally hop to second and third position is easier for some than others. If you find it difficult, just think how much more successful you can be by working on this skill.

Here are some trigger questions to ask yourself that will help with this mental shift:

'How does this person see me?'
'If I were him, what would I be thinking?'
'If I were a film director filming this, what sort of film would it be?'

To achieve your goals you need to remain flexible and be sensitive to both your own position and that of others.

There is a scene in the play *Fiddler on the Roof* where a judge is presiding over a legal dispute. The first party argued his case very eloquently. The judge was impressed. 'You are right!' he shouted.

'Just a minute,' said the second party, who then argued his case just as convincingly.

'Of course,' said the judge. 'You are right!'

The clerk of the court coughed politely. 'Excuse me, sir,' he said, 'they both cannot be right.'

The judge thought for a moment. 'No, of course not,' he said. 'You're right.'

13

VALUES –
WHAT IS IMPORTANT?

Values are what is important to us in our lives. They give us directions and underpin our goals. Sometimes decisions are difficult because, like the judge, we agree with both sides of a dilemma. Congruence is acting in accordance with your values. You may see the customer's viewpoint and appreciate the company viewpoint, but in the end *you* have to decide. To be pressured into going against your values and beliefs is a certain way of losing your internal state. If you do not believe in the pricing policy of the company, the quality of its products or the value that it offers, each sale you make will create internal conflict which can, in the extreme, affect your sleep patterns, health and relationships both in and out of work.

Goals are about what you want to have. Values are about who you want to be. Criteria are values applied to a particular context. What is important to us in home life is likely to be different from what is important to us in professional life. Just as we move towards values like freedom and love, so we will move away from such states as humiliation, guilt and rejection. These are our moving away values, the things it is important for us to avoid. As with goals, it is much better to work towards what we want than spend time avoiding what we do not want.

MONEY

Money usually ranks fairly high in most people's hierarchy of values. Yet money has no value in itself. It is valuable as a means to an end, as a means of achieving other more important things: comfort, security, happiness, love, health.

Take a few moments to think about and note down answers to these questions:

- *What yearly salary would it take for you to feel financially secure?*

The higher this is, the more you are likely to value security.

- *What is the difference between this figure and your fixed basic salary?*
  If you work on a commission basis, what fixed salary would you be willing to have to compensate for loss of commission?

  The higher this is, the more you value your ability to determine your own income.

- *Suppose you were offered your dream job: ideal working conditions, doing just what you wanted in the professional area you were most interested in. Your salary is guaranteed the same as it is now. You can negotiate a bonus. What would it be?*

  (If you are already in your ideal job, congratulations!)

- *Suppose that one of the conditions of this offer was that you had to work in the same job for five years. Would this change the bonus you would want?*
  What about ten years?

  The higher you set your bonus under these circumstances, the more you value your freedom to move.

- *Suppose you were offered your nightmare job. A job you really hate. Your salary will be the same as in your existing job. What extra bonus would you want to negotiate for you to take the nightmare job?*
  What would that money do for you to compensate for the nightmare job?

For some people millions are not enough.

(If you are already in your nightmare job, are you being adequately compensated?)

You can use money as a useful index of what you value about your work by asking the general question:

'If I had to give up ... in my work, how much extra salary would I want as compensation?'

The larger the compensation, the more you value that aspect of your work.

So money is a useful measure of how much you value other things, it has no value in itself. You might build a hierarchy of values by setting how much monetary compensation you would want to forego each of your positive values.

HIERARCHY OF VALUES

All your values are important – and some are more important than others. Very often decisions are difficult because both sides fulfil some values. Which are most important? Without some way of ranking your values, you would be paralysed. This next section is about finding out what is most important to you. Then you can align your goals with your values.

What is most important to you about your profession? This process will help you find out.

1. Think of three important, significant experiences in your work. For example, a promotion, closing a big sale or meeting a particular customer. Make sure they are actual specific experiences. Write them down.

2. Think about the first experience. What is it about this that makes it important for you now? It may not have seemed important at the time. Write down some key phrases for each experience. For example, if the experience was closing a sale, then some important elements might be excitement, sense of achievement, praise, large commission, celebration and congratulations from your friends.

3. Take each of these key words you have written down and ask, what is important about those things? Chase up each word and write some key words about each key word. You are likely to have about a dozen words now.

   For example, with the example of closing a sale, you might now have values like self-belief, confidence, success, self-esteem. Taking each of *these* words, expand the list again. For example, success could go to recognition, financial security and winning.

4. Do this with each of the original three experiences. This will give you a list of between a dozen and 30 words. Note the ones that are duplicated, as they are likely to be important, but only count them once.

5. Now, taking *all* these key words for all three experiences that you have written since the beginning, if you had to choose six that are the most important to you, which ones would they be?

   The way to find this out is to review all your criteria words and decide, if you had to lose one, which one would it be? This criterion that you decide to lose is bottom in your hierarchy. Now, of the remaining criteria, if you had to lose one more, which would it be? This one is second from bottom. Keep doing this until you have only six left.

6. Now it becomes more difficult. These final six will be your most important criteria about your professional work. Continue to rank them. If you had to lose one of those six, which one would you lose? Then of the five left, which one would you lose? Carry on until you have arranged your six top values in order of importance.

An example of what you might finish with would be:

1. Freedom
2. Love
3. Wealth
4. Relationships
5. Security
6. Being appreciated

The question now is: Are these values being met?

RULES

What has to happen?

Your values and criteria come with rules attached for their fulfilment, called *criterial equivalents* in NLP. You need to find your own, just as you need to find those of your customers.

Imagine asking two salespeople, 'What has to happen for you to feel successful?'

Salesperson one says, '£40,000, a year, a house outside the city and a BMW 525i.'

Salesperson two says, '£80,000 a year, quitting smoking and getting my weight down to 76 kilos.'

Success is self-determined. You set the rules.

Ask yourself the question for each of your six values, 'What has to happen for me to get ... (value)...?' This will give you your rules.

Are your rules satisfying, empowering and realistic?

Make sure the criterial equivalents satisfy you. We are not saying, feel happy by lowering your sights. However, check that your rules empower rather than limit you.

In general, there are three cases where rules are not empowering.

1. They are impossible to meet. Rules have to be realistic or you set yourself up for failure.

2. They are dependent on something or someone that is out of your control.

   Here there is a danger that you will get into the *blame frame*, where your happiness becomes the responsibility of others rather than yourself. This gives others tremendous power over you in a world that is not noted for its kindness or fairness.

   The key phrase to watch for in the blame frame is: *'If only* such and such were to happen, or so and so would do something … *then* I would be happy.'

3. They give you many ways to feel bad and only a few ways to feel good. This is like a customer who has decided that only a Pantone 601 blue three-quarter-sized Gizmo delivered tomorrow can possibly meet his need. When your rules are very highly specified, you are difficult to satisfy. Apply your sales skill to your values in the same way you apply them to a customer's need. These rules are only one way of meeting the value. What other ways are there?

BENEFITS AND VALUES

If sales is a win–win transaction, what do you win? Separate the benefits of a particular sale from the benefits of the job. A particular sale will give you commission, a feeling of success, self-esteem and praise. Work in sales has many benefits:

- You can apply your skills to many different kinds of product, so you have freedom to move into different market areas.
- You control your income to a greater extent than in many jobs.
- You help people get what they want.
- You meet many different people.

One final question. We are discussing selling almost as if it is a thing, but it is an activity, it is something you do. When you think about selling, do you think about it simply as something you do or do you say 'I am a salesperson'? When you say that, sales is part of your identity as a person.

How far are your values being met? If you are working for a company where business practices are aligned with your standards and values, you are either lucky, very astute at choosing an employer or you own the company. It is unlikely that all are being met, so, like a customer, you can trade off one against another. However, if none of the values are being well met, then you might consider looking at another product.

Often, messages about company values can be mixed. For example, many insurance salespeople are being pressured to improve the quality of their business, that is to say, to make certain that what is sold is exactly right for the customer. But if a salesperson is then pressured for quantity of business, which may well impact on the quality, they are left chasing two different and conflicting standards. If a dog chases two rabbits it tends to catch neither.

When confronted by pressures to go against your own values, your options are limited. You can keep your head down, keep strong and hope to produce enough business to shield you from the pressure. You can try to sell your values upwards. You can prove your values work by outperforming others. Or, and this is the most common approach, you can be more specific about choosing your next employer. Seek a company that meets your values. Interview them to make sure their values meet yours.

MOTIVATION AND WORKING STYLES

14

Motivation is about influencing yourself to do what you have to do. In the Old Bazaar, motivation was about manipulating yourself to do what you had to do. Given that we have many different parts, not all necessarily wanting to do the work in hand, how do you influence, as opposed to manipulate, yourself? The ways you use will be reflections of the ways others influence you.

The methods we suggest may be very different to those of more familiar motivational trainings which tend to wallpaper over dissatisfaction and are a poor substitute for congruence.

The carrot and the stick

Debate has raged over the years between these two approaches that seem at first to be conflicting: the 'carrot' and the 'stick'. How do you motivate people? Give them a goal and rewards. This is the 'carrot' approach. Punish them if they fail. This is the stick approach. They both work.

What kind of approach do you use with yourself? Do you think of working towards what you want or are you driven by the unpleasant consequences of not doing the task? If it is the latter, then you are also likely to leave things to the last minute, when the consequences loom large on your time line and can no longer be ignored. This approach can be difficult and stressful, and can make life difficult for others who work with you.

Working towards goals and rewards is generally more pleasant and less stressful. Successful salespeople are nearly always motivated towards reward.

The dictator and the siren

Another motivational strategy that does not work very well is known as the dictator.

The dictator is that voice in your head that tells you that you *must* do something. You *should* do it, you *have to* do it, why don't you get on and *DO IT!* The natural consequence of being nagged like this is to resist. The voice is, however, really trying to help you. Its intentions are golden but its method is crass.

Have you noticed how annoying the sound and tonality of the voice can be? It is not just the words, it's the way you say them to yourself. Some people who have listened to their inner voice closely say it sounds suspiciously like one of their parents.

The dictator is not a good motivation strategy. If you have one like it, change it to the siren strategy, which works much better. To do this, you need to do two things.

First, change the tonality of the voice. Make it seductive, sexy, alluring, a pleasure to listen to.

Secondly, change the words it uses. Ban several words from your internal vocabulary: 'have to', 'must', 'should' and 'ought'. These words are known as 'modal operators'. They are not very pleasant and not very effective. If they were, you would not have to keep using them.

Replace these modal operators with '*I can.*' So '*I must* make this call' becomes '*I can* make this call.' 'I can' is more permissive and empowering.

Maybe you use these modal operators in the negative: 'must not', 'should not', 'ought not'. These set boundaries. Ask yourself the same freeing question you would ask your customers when you hear these words: 'What would happen if I did...?'

Find out the real constraints behind the words and the possible consequences. They may be less important than you think.

Add this siren strategy to a carrot strategy for even better results. It can make work a pleasure.

Doing and done

The third strategy that does not work well is to imagine yourself actually doing the work. For a chore that you do not particularly enjoy, imagine what it will be like with the task *done*. Feel good in advance. Anticipate the pleasure of getting the task out of the way and how this will open up other opportunities. See the task completed in your mind's eye. If the task is a pleasant one, imagine doing the work. Feel the pleasure in advance that you will get in doing that task. Then do it for real.

Finally, you do not have to do the work all at once, you can divide it into smaller tasks. Remember too that if you think of a task as part of a larger goal, it is more motivating and then the smaller task is easier.

WORKING STYLES

Another way to think of motivation is to know your own working styles so you can arrange your work to your strengths. There is so much we might do and so much information we could pay attention to, we have all evolved some filters to screen out what we are not interested in. You will see the same patterns in your customers. These patterns are called *metaprograms* in NLP and they have been developed for use in business by Rodger Bailey as the Language and Behaviour (LAB) Profile.

Metaprograms are very simple. For example, think of a glass full of water. Now imagine drinking half of it. What is left? Is the glass half full or half empty? Both. No one in their right mind would have an argument about that. Some people look at a job and think of the advantages, others look at the same job and see all the disadvantages. Neither of these patterns is better than the other, just different.

Some working patterns may seem obvious. These are likely to be your own. Others may appear crazy – that is because they are the patterns of others.

Two cautions here. First, these patterns can change by context. In other words, a person may be very pessimistic in his professional life and see nothing but half empty glasses. (This is sometimes called 'downside planning' and insurance companies employ a lot of such people to ask the question, 'What *could* go wrong here?') Yet in his home life, the same person may see a lot of half full glasses.

Secondly, very few people show these patterns in the extreme, they exist more as tendencies, preferences about how we view the world.

Proactive–reactive

The first pattern is about action. A *proactive* person initiates action. He jumps in and does it. Proactive people share the slogan with Nike sportswear: Just Do It. The reactive person will hold back, think about it and wait for others.

There is the joke about the strongly reactive person who was deeply religious and wanted to make a lot of money. He then planned to give it away to charitable causes and do good works. So he prayed to his god. He prayed religiously for years and nothing happened. He became disheartened. One night his god appeared to him in a dream. 'Listen,' said God, 'meet me halfway, OK? Buy the lottery ticket.'

Selling is mostly a proactive profession. You go out and contact people. Proactive customers are more likely to impulse buy, reactive customers to hang back and think about it (and maybe never buy).

Think about your company. It may be full of proactive people, but it might have a reactive culture due to work pressure. It is not unusual for companies to extol the virtues of proactivity and then lurch from crisis to crisis responding to short-term emergencies while salespeople, hired for their proactivity, have to react to organisational problems.

Towards–away from

This is a pattern we have met many times in different guises. *Towards* people are goal motivated. They like to move towards something worth having. They stay focused on their goals. They respond well to challenges where achievement will bring good feeling and rewards. Trips abroad, nights out and other promotions will motivate the *towards* person, as will recognition and status. The traditional system of sales charts, monthly rewards and striving for monthly figures is completely geared to *towards* people. Customers who are *towards* will buy to make the gain rather than to avoid a problem.

People who show the *away from* pattern are motivated to avoid loss. They notice difficulties and are particularly good at identifying and solving problems in advance. Prizes and recognition are not so important to *away from* people; threat, fear of dismissal and loss of face are more effective motivators.

It is the old argument about the carrot and the stick – which is the better motivator? The answer is either, depending on whom you are motivating.

A high percentage of salespeople are *towards* people. When dealing with customers they will focus heavily on the benefits their product offers. However, if the customer is *away from*, then discussions on the losses involved in not buying the product may produce quicker decisions. Life assurance can offer either comfort when you retire or the avoidance of hardship to the family should you die. Knowing whether a customer is either *towards* or *away from* will dictate the emphasis you place on the two extremes.

Many *towards* salespeople find themselves working for managers who· expect everyone to respond to an *away from* management style. That is to say, the managers use threat as their main motivation. If you are in this position, it is even more important that you set your own goals and to work towards something positive. Otherwise the management style will drain your motivation and energy.

Again, look at your company. Does it encourage a *towards* attitude for its salespeople, yet react to the market and circumstances to avoid loss? Does it take the market opportunities?

General–detail

General people are more comfortable looking at the overall framework. They like to see the whole project, they think and understand conceptually. They tend to talk in global terms. They would not attempt a jigsaw puzzle without first getting a feel and understanding of the picture on the front of the box. If you give them part of a task they become demotivated if not allowed to see where their part fits into the whole. They can concentrate more on 'what' they are looking to achieve as opposed to the 'how'. They often leave out steps in a sequence.

Detail people build towards the big picture by putting smaller pieces together. To them, an overall concept is not only unimportant, it can be a distraction. This characteristic may lead to difficulties in establishing priorities. They might be found cleaning the life boats while the ship goes down.

Imagine a *detail* salesperson meeting a *general* client. There is a problem if the salesperson insists on talking about the detail of the product and the specifics of how it will be delivered, installed and commissioned, when all the customer wants to know is what are the overall benefits, the costs and general points. Conversely, if it is the customer who is *detail* and the salesperson *general*, there can be frustration on the part of the customer because he does not receive enough information on which to base his decision and confusion on behalf of the salesperson because she has given a perfectly adequate overview.

Generally speaking, the higher the level you are selling to, the more general the way you have to frame your product. This is one reason why some salespeople do well with large sales at board level – it comes to them more naturally to paint the big picture.

Options–procedure

This pattern is particularly important in sales. *Options* people wants to have choice and develop alternatives, often compulsively. They are excellent at developing systems, but poor at following them, however good the systems are. Freedom to choose and be different is important to them. An *options* person will never follow a script to the letter, however good it is.

Procedures people on the other hand are good at following routines. They are more concerned about how to do something than why they are doing it. Without a routine, they may feel stuck. Many jobs in the business world are only performed successfully by procedures: accounting, computer programming, piloting aircraft, for example. Money is made in business by following procedures that work (and by inventing other ones that work as well or better).

This creates an interesting paradox in business, particularly in sales. Most sales training is procedural. A script is very procedural. However, although sales training is designed to develop procedures, it generally also tends to put over the idea that the options pattern is better. The sales profession tends to attract options people who are then encouraged to follow procedures.

We are aiming in our sales approach to give a strong enough frame within which you can be as creative as you wish. A good script gives you a flexible framework within which you can be creative.

Internal–external

How do you know you have done a good piece of work? Think about the question for a moment. There are two extreme categories of answer. The first is: 'I just know.' This is the answer given by *internal* people. They have their standards and use them to compare actions and to decide what to do. Strongly internal people insist on deciding for themselves and will resist the decisions of others on their behalf. They are often labelled as 'stubborn', they may have difficulty accepting management and need very little supervision. Sometimes strongly internal people feel uncomfortable about influencing customers. They want them to make up their mind for themselves with the minimum of external influence. This is not selling.

The answer from a strongly external person would be 'When other people say so.' External people need a management style with lots of external motivation, praise and guidance.

Both the carrot and the stick management motivation strategies are external. *External* people need others to supply standards for decision and action. They are much more amenable to feedback and will follow standards very easily. *External* people need to be managed and need feedback on how they are working.

Most people have a balance of the two directions: they have internal standards and also value external feedback.

Match–mismatch

This pattern is about comparison, about noticing what is the same and what is different.

Mismatchers notice differences. They like to know what is different about products and are very aware of differences in general. They also like change and become easily bored if things stay the same. They often change jobs rapidly.

Customers who show this pattern like to know a product is 'new' and 'different'.

Matchers notice what stays the same about people, situations, events. People who match also like to stay in the same work. They like the familiar.

The in-between pattern is the most common: sameness with exception. Sales is a good example. You do the same kind of work, but with different people every day.

Independent–proximity–co-operative

This is a pattern about working relationships. Many sales jobs attract *independent* people. They enjoy and are good at working on their own, they are productive and take responsibility for the results.

Proximity people like to work around other people. They work well supervising or being supervised by others. *Proximity* people make good sales managers and good salespeople as they get rapport quite easily with others.

Co-operative people work best when they are working alongside others, sharing responsibility. They work best in teams. The best sales teams have co-operative and proximity people, which is why the best sales teams do not necessarily contain the best individual salespeople.

These are the main metaprogram patterns. They are tendencies rather than all or nothing patterns. They are descriptions, not explanations, and if you find yourself fitting closely to one pattern, that does not mean you do not have a choice about what you do.

You are not your behaviour and your metaprograms do not fix your behaviour. No pattern is absolutely better than another, it depends what you want to do.

Software is available that allows you to explore these patterns in greater detail (see Consultancy section).

In general, sales culture encourages salespeople who are towards, proactive, external and proximity. And as we have seen, it also gives them mixed messages. What is important is that you are congruent with the work you are doing. We will look at this next.

15

MENTAL PREPARATION

CONGRUENCE CHECK

Congruence in your work is the alignment of goals and values. When you are congruent, you can be confident you are competent. Your congruence affects the customers, who, fairly or not, link their feelings for the salesperson to their feelings for the product. If they do separate the product from its representative, they buy despite and not because of him. Would you buy a weight control course from a doughnut munching, 18 stone salesperson?

It is also important to be congruent about particular parts or elements of your work. This section shows how you test for your own congruence. You can use this congruence check in any area of your life.

First, remember some time when you were completely committed to some task or goal. It can be anything, not necessarily connected to selling. As you think back into that situation, see what you saw in that situation, hear what you heard and feel what you felt. Now be aware of how your body feels. What is it like to be committed? For many people it is a 'gut feeling'. For others it is the particular tone of voice they hear in their mind. Find out your unique signal. Get to know that feeling. It is impossible to fake. You cannot fool yourself. You may get a graded signal. The stronger the feeling the more congruent you are.

The second step is to get an incongruence signal.

Remember a time when you were *not* fully committed to some task or project. You were incongruent. A 'yes, but' situation. What does that feel like? What does your body feel like, what pictures and sounds do you have internally? Many people hear a doubting voice tone in their mind in this situation. This signal is your friend. It is warning you that there is something not yet right about the situation.

Now think about the element of your work you are checking for congruence. For example, ask yourself, 'Am I congruent about this meeting?' and be sensitive to the signal your body sends back. You can use the absence of the congruence signal or the presence of the incongruence signal as a warning that you are not fully prepared. If this is so, you will have to ask yourself some questions and negotiate with yourself as if you were both salesperson and customer, for clearly there are parts of you that are not 'sold' on what you are about to do.

What would you have to do before you could feel congruent about the task?
Do you have adequate preparation time?
Does it put you under pressure in your life?
Is this a place where you need to say no?
Do you know the product well enough?

Identify what you have to do to become congruent. Very often it is some extra preparation or a special condition you need to attend to.

MEETING PREPARATION

The success of a sales meeting is dependent on the quality of the preparation you do. There are two types of preparation. Attending to both will help your congruence and effectiveness in the meeting.

1. The practical issues – such as making sure you have the literature and you arrive on time. Many managers would expect no more of you.
2. Mental preparation. Mental rehearsal is one absolutely consistent action of all top performers in every field we know of.

Mental rehearsal means going through in your mind how you want the meeting to be. Give your mind images of success and it will create the imagined success in the real world. We all know how our expectations create self-fulfilling prophecies. Think you will fail and you probably will. Plan for success and, if it is at all possible, you will achieve it.

Mental rehearsal for success

This is a simple process of mental rehearsal used by many top performers.

- Imagine the scene of your greatest success, a time when you felt good about what you were doing, you were confident and everything went very well. It does not have to be a sales meeting.
- Secondly, you want to know the qualities of this scene. Pay close attention to the scene you have conjured up in your mind and describe it to yourself. Look at your mental image:

  Are you seeing yourself in the picture or are you in it, seeing through your own eyes?

  How big is your mental picture?

  How bright is it?

  Is it a moving or a still picture?

  Is it in colour or in black and white?

  Where in space is the picture, all around? To one side?

  Is the picture focused or fuzzy?

  Is it two- or three-dimensional?

  What else do you notice about the picture?

- Write down these characteristics of your confident mental image. These distinctions of how you see the picture are called *visual submodalities* in NLP.

  Now pay attention to any sounds in your memory of that scene.

  Do you hear voices, sounds or both?

  Whereabouts do the sounds come from?

  How loud are the sounds?

  Is there a rhythm?

  Are they louder or softer than normal?

  If there are voices, what are they saying and in what tonality?

- Write down these characteristics. They are the auditory submodalities.

Your mind clothes its images of success in a certain way. To mentally rehearse for success in the future, think about the imagined scene in the same way as your success in the past. What you have just discovered is how your brain codes your successes.

If you do not believe us, remember the scene of one of your less pleasant experiences, one you would prefer to forget. Notice how the picture is different. It may be darker, smaller, in a different place. The sound quality is probably different. If some gremlin were to shuffle these two, you could tell just by looking and listening which was the successful one, without hearing any of the words spoken. Of course the actual scene and who is in it will be different, but the way you think about it will be different as well.

Now, think about your upcoming meeting in the way you just thought about your success. If your successful memory was big and bright, mentally rehearse the meeting as a big, bright picture. Fit the upcoming meeting into the frame of the successful memory. Now watch yourself in the meeting as you would a video film. Create and edit the video as you go along. You are the star. See yourself there. Run it in just the way you want it to go. Listen to the soundtrack. Notice the customer's responses. Anticipate difficult questions. Watch yourself easily and confidently getting your goal. Watch it all happen through to the end until you are completely satisfied.

Now, when you are satisfied with the inner film you have created, step inside it. This is called *associating into* your mental image. See and hear the meeting as if you were there. Before, you were a fly on the wall making sure everything was just right. Now be in there acting the way you have decided, speaking in the way you have prepared. If at any time you are dissatisfied, step out of your mental video and edit the film until you are satisfied. Then step back in again. To get the most from mental rehearsal, you have to be associated in your mental movie.

What you cannot do of course with this exercise is to influence what the customer is going to say and do directly, but you can change the way you behave, and therefore his response when you are face to face.

Now plan the meeting from each of the three viewpoints. Place as many chairs as there will be people in roughly the position you would expect them to be in during your actual meeting. Then sit in the seat that you will occupy. Although the office environment, desk layout and general geography will be different in this rehearsal than it will be in the real thing, you can pretend your way into making it as realistic as possible. Then plan the meeting from your point of view, from first position. Use the insights you have from the previous exercise. Establish what you are looking to achieve, how you will know if you've achieved it, what manner you're going to adopt, how you will structure the meeting and anything else it seems useful to plan.

Once you've gathered the information from first position, move to the customer's chair and think yourself into being her. Now plan the meeting from this second position. What are my wants, needs and values *as customer*? What am I looking for? Aspects and thoughts will come to you regarding the customer's approach to the meeting that would never have been available had you just thought about the meeting from your own position.

Having gathered the second position information, stand to the side

of the chairs and take on the persona of the playwright or film director and predict what is likely to happen between these two people with
the plans and intentions you have gleaned from your first and second
positions. It is likely that by this time you will be able to give yourself
some sound advice on how to improve your approach. Be your own
coach. With that advice, return to the first position chair and replan
the meeting. You can of course do this in your head without the
chairs.

Preparing a good emotional state

The most important factor in your success at a sales meeting will be
your emotional state. How do you want to feel? Think of the principles of goal-setting. If you think 'I don't want to feel *nervous*', guess
how you will feel?

Many salespeople would answer that they want to feel confident.
Confidence comes first from good preparation. Ask yourself, 'Do I
deserve to succeed?' You need to know your material. If you do not,
you are quite right to feel uncomfortable. The other factor to think
about is how many times you have to succeed to feel confident. Once?
Twice? Three times? More than that? Never? Different people have
different answers. Think about this question if you have to prove it to
yourself every time you go out.

There is a simple process that will allow you to feel resourceful or
confident or however you want to feel in a difficult meeting. It works
on what is known as 'the roller-coaster principle'. Imagine you are on
a roller-coaster at the top of a ride (or any fairground ride if you have
never been on a roller-coaster). Now, relive the experience of going
down that ride, seeing what you saw, hearing what you heard and
whoaaaa ... feeling what you felt. Now, you are not actually on a roller-
coaster, right? Yet you can recapture a great deal of the feelings.
Imagined and relived memories create real feelings in the here and
now. All you need do to use this principle to your advantage is to
remember a time when you did feel confident and use those feelings.
It does not have to be in the same situation of a sales meeting. It can
be in any situation. It is the feeling you want, not the situation. If you
think you have never felt confident, are you really sure? Positive? Are
you absolutely confident you have never felt confident? If so, use *that*
feeling of certainty.

The first step, then, is to think of a situation in the past when you
felt as you wish to feel in the forthcoming meeting.

Go back to that memory as strongly as you can.

See what you saw then, hear what you heard then and get the feeling as strongly as you can. Then come back into the present moment.

Next, decide what association or trigger you want to remind you of that feeling. In NLP this is called an *anchor*. We can make any associations we want to bring the feelings we want, instead of randomly responding to environmental anchors. Examples of anchors we respond to every day are red traffic lights, the telephone ringing and a police siren. Advertisers try to anchor their product to good feelings by clever use of images and sound. You can create anchors for yourself. One sales manager turned a picture that was hanging on the wall in his office upside down. Every time it caught his eye, it reminded him that he could see things a little differently and not be so predictable, if he chose. Another hung a horseshoe on his wall. When asked, 'Surely you don't believe in that superstitious stuff about horseshoes and good luck?' he would reply, 'Of course not!' 'Why do you have it then?' was the next question. Then he would say, 'Because it works!'

Choose your anchors:

Visual – something you can see in your mind's eye, for example a symbol or the scene of your remembered experience.
Auditory – one sound or word you can say to yourself. If it is a word, make sure the tonality expresses the confidence you want to feel.
Kinesthetic – one small inconspicuous gesture you can make. Some people use a clenched fist or touching two fingers together.

Next, go back and fully experience the resourceful state that you want. See what you saw, hear what you heard and feel your full body sense. It can help if you put your body into the same position as you were then (if appropriate). When the resourceful feeling is at its height, connect your three anchors to the feeling – see the picture, hear the sound and make the gesture. Then come out of that state and think of something else.

Test your anchors. See the picture, hear the sound and make the gesture and notice how this brings back the resourceful feeling. If you are not satisfied, go back to the previous step and link them again to the resourceful feeling. Do this as many times as you need to, so that the anchors do bring back the resourceful feeling each time.

Mentally rehearse the meeting using your associations. You can use them to get yourself into a resource state at the start of the meeting and as a recovery strategy if things go badly during the meeting.

Anchoring and using your resourceful states is a skill and it gets easier the more you practise. For many people it works dramatically first time. We live in a culture that believes feelings are involuntary, created by other people. This 'roller-coaster' technique is one way of gaining some control and choice over what you feel, instead of being at the mercy of the situation.

MENTAL DEBRIEFING

Everyone makes mistakes; the trick is to learn from them so you do not make the same mistake twice. This section completes the cycle by reviewing and learning from the meeting. Do this within 24 hours of the meeting while the memory is fresh. The process will take about ten minutes.

Relax in a quiet place where you are unlikely to be disturbed. Replay the whole meeting like a video, seeing what you saw, hearing what you heard, feeling what you felt. Do not attempt to remember the whole meeting, replay it like the edited highlights of a sports match. As you do this, you will notice places where you would like more choices. Remember these places. When you have finished reviewing the edited highlights, go back to each of the places where you would like some more choices and stop your mental video. This point may be where you did something that hindered the sale. It may be where you were OK and you would like to be better. It may be you did fine, but you would like to explore a few more choices.

After you have stopped the video, jump out mentally, take a detached viewpoint and watch yourself in the meeting at that point. Now creatively edit the tape sequence and watch yourself doing something else, something better, more appropriate. When you are satisfied, mentally jump in again and rehearse yourself doing this new choice in the situation. Enjoy acting what might have been. As you act it out, check that it works well. If you discover something is still wrong, come out, think of another alternative, watch yourself doing it and go through the process again, until you are completely satisfied from both viewpoints: the viewpoint of you watching yourself and the viewpoint of you actually doing it.

It did not happen then of course, but next time...

Go through the whole meeting like this and learn as much as

possible. The key question to ask yourself during this process is: 'What would I do differently next time?'

Take your mental video and store it somewhere safe. You do not have to be aware of it all the time for the new choices to affect your performance.

Development plans

Hopefully, the company you work for accepts responsibility for providing time and money to support your further skill training and development, and your career progression. Unfortunately, many do not. Training can be seen as a cost rather than an investment. And where there is a budget, it is often focused on training the skills you need now, in your present position, with little thought to developing the skills that will be useful in your next job along the career path.

No matter how well your company supports you with training and development, it makes sense to take responsibility for it yourself. You then have control.

Any job is a combination of different skills. These skills are like links in a chain that join together to make the finished product. Unfortunately, not many of us are good at all the aspects of our work, all the links in our chain. Some of the skills we need take a little more work. Some people try to compensate for the weaker links by making a strength stronger. If a sales person is not good at cold calling he might become excellent at closing, the logic being that although not a lot of opportunities are opened up by him, those that are get closed.

There is a plan of skill building exercises at the end of this book and trainings to take it further if you wish, listed in the Consultancy section. Training is about building skills in a safe situation, so they become second nature in a real situation with a customer. As we practise more and more, we have to pay less and less conscious attention to what we do. From conscious incompetence we move to unconscious competence, when we do not have to think about what we do, we just do it. At this level you are the master at what you choose to do.

PART FOUR

SALES MANAGEMENT

16

LEADERSHIP

In management your sales skills are necessary, but are no longer sufficient. To be able to create an empowering environment where people want to produce quantity and quality of business requires abilities some of us may never even have thought about until given the manager's hat, the title and instructions to get on with it.

We will focus on three aspects of becoming a 'successful' manager:

• what NLP can bring to effective management
• applying self-management skills in an organisational setting
• the implications of the New Bazaar for sales management

As a manager, you need a wide organisational view of selling. You need to appreciate the first position: the salesperson's viewpoint. You need to be aware of second position: the customer's viewpoint; and you particularly need to be able to take a third position: looking at the total process. In many respects, management uses the same organisational skills we have already looked at – managing goals, setting priorities, breaking the goals down to manageable pieces and understanding the resources to deliver those pieces – but writ large across a wider area.

Sales managers often earn less than some of the salespeople they manage. They work longer hours under greater stress for less recognition. Whereas a salesperson can focus clearly on what she wants to get out of the job and work towards personal goals, managers must be more aware of corporate need and goals, and the well-being of their sales team. As a manager you can no longer be selfish and measure achievement purely by how you, personally, have gained. Your awareness, interest and concern need to spread to every corner of the business.

A sales manager needs also to strike the right balance between reactivity – responding to events and emergencies – and proactivity –

initiating action. It will be the model that you set that others will follow.

Many people seek a management position because it just seems the natural progression to take. Some fancy the chance of having other people do what they say for a change. It is important to be clear about your motives in seeking a management role. If you are made up to a manager and then find you don't like it, it's difficult to go back to selling within the same organisation. Ask yourself:

'What do I really want out of sales management?'

Think about your goals if you have not done so already in the last section.

Then ask yourself:

'What is really important to me about sales management?'

Be clear about your own values as a sales manager.

LEADERSHIP

Of a great leader, the people will say, 'We did it ourselves.'

Lao Tzu

First and foremost, a manager is a leader. A manager cuts through the forest to make progress. A leader also climbs a tree, looks round and could well shout, 'Wrong jungle!' You lead others, and to do that well, you need to lead yourself. Managers face two main tasks: first, to develop and clarify exactly what the company is trying to achieve; and secondly to create an empowering environment where the people they manage can use their personal resources and qualities to the fullest extent to perform at their best.

Your greatest resources are your people. Salespeople are very valuable. They need to be looked after. Always treat your employees exactly how you want them to treat your best customers – they will. Salespeople cost a lot to train and recruit, and good ones are hard to come by. Leadership is increasingly about team-building, getting very different people to pull in the same direction, so their differences become a source of strength and not dissension. A good leader develops others so they too can be leaders.

Quality leadership comes from congruence. When your goals and values are aligned, you become more powerful and are able to achieve more. Teams pull apart if the members have conflicting interests. In the same way, it is hard to succeed if your internal parts are pulling in different directions. In athletics, the winner is usually the competitor whose whole body is working towards his goal. The slightest drawback can make a difference, perhaps only a tenth of a second, yet that is all that separates the winner from the runners up.

Leadership is an emotive word, and tends to conjure up military visions of charisma and battles won and lost. Now, people are more likely to march with you if you share their values rather than if you order them to. The best leaders share attributes like intelligence, commitment, energy, integrity and credibility. Salespeople in the New Bazaar need exactly these qualities in their leaders.

A leader is at the service of his colleagues. The old pyramid shape of management is being turned on its head. Instead of the base of the pyramid all leading up to, and supporting, the manager at the top, the pyramid balances on its point. The managers, from the CEO downwards, serve the people beneath them. The organisation serves the customer.

Beliefs

What you believe about people will determine how you manage them. Although we do not usually think of beliefs as resources, here are four helpful beliefs. They are basic principles of NLP. They may or may not be true, it is impossible to say. Act as if they were true and notice the results you get. Our beliefs have the nature of self-fulfilling prophecies. Whether you believe you can or you can't – *you're right*.

1. *We all act with a positive intention.*
   This means that all our actions are completely understandable within our frame of reference. We all make mistakes, which are easy to see in hindsight. But however stupid our actions may appear later or from the outside, given the beliefs and ideas we had, they seemed sensible at the time, the best choice. Someone blundering round shooting at people with an imaginary gun looks crazy, until you notice he is wearing a virtual reality helmet. We can create some very bizarre realities in our head without the help of a such a headset!

2. *We all have the resources we need to do the job or we can acquire them.*
Without this belief, delegating and giving responsibility is nerve-racking. You have to trust. Micro-managing and reluctance to delegate gives a message to your people that they are incompetent and is the fast track to an executive ulcer.

3. *No one comes to work to do a bad job.*
This is closely related to the other two. If you believe people want to work, are honest and keen to excel, you will create an environment in which people are free and encouraged to perform.

4. *There is no failure, only feedback.*
Failure is a way of describing results you do not want. Failure seems very final. Think instead of keeping your goal in mind and aiming for it. Use the results you get as feedback to adjust what you do. Learn from feedback about what to do next.

Unless you are superman (and that is an awful responsibility) you will make mistakes. However, a leader is flexible and utilises the results even if they are not exactly what he wanted. He can cope with the unexpected, even turn it to advantage. Circumstances change, even from day to day and your management style needs to change accordingly. A sudden drop in performance, a top performer experiencing personal problems, a change in company policy or strategy will all change the way you handle your people.

Motivation

A manager motivates and inspires his sales team. When you lead people, you also motivate them. How can you congruently motivate people in a way that acknowledges their goals and values? Not the way that some managers handle their teams – as though they were going out to play football. They get them together at eight in the morning, lampoon and threaten the poor performers, encourage and excite the others and send them out like clockwork toys wound up to breaking point. This form of motivation is not suitable for long-term performance. It may work for the weight-lifter whose job is done in 10 seconds, but for salespeople who will be talking with many customers over the week, adrenalin rushes are not the way to motivate.

Motivation is also often confused with judging progress. Salespeople are encouraged to compare themselves with others who are doing much better. This is supposed to be motivating, the positive intention

of the message being, 'You too could be like this.' However, this type of comparison just makes people feel bad. It reminds people of school where teachers said things like, 'Why can't you be like Johnny? He's so good.' The answer to this is, 'I don't want to be like Johnny, I want to be myself, and if you keep holding up Johnny as a role model, I am going to get to dislike him, because the thought of him makes me feel bad.' So the comparison form of motivation is not only ineffective but divisive.

The way you motivate yourself is likely to be the way you try to motivate others. We have already talked about the carrot and the stick model of motivation. If you are a *towards* person, you will motivate others by reward: the carrot philosophy. An *away from* person is likely to motivate others by threat of punishment: the stick philosophy.

This stick approach was taken to an extreme by the manager who gathered his sales team on Monday morning and said, 'I am firing all of you now. You have until Friday afternoon to persuade me you deserve your jobs back.' This style of management creates bad feelings and becomes 'bad news management'.

A 'bad news manager' is one whose very appearance is an anchor for trouble. These are the ones who only want to know what went wrong and the mistakes you have made. You only hear from them when in trouble. 'You'll know you are doing all right if you do not hear from me' is the common message. But a manager who is a leader will encourage proactivity and the personal and professional development of his or her colleagues. This development will be internally generated and not coerced through incentive schemes.

Both carrot and stick are external inducements. They bring us back to the Old Bazaar, when selling was a battle against customer reluctance, customers were the enemy, battlements to be stormed and incongruent salespeople needed external motivation – pressure, threats or extra rewards.

If you want a graphic metaphor for the long-term effect of this system of motivation, try this experiment. Lightly grease the floor of a microwave oven with sunflower oil. Position as many grapes as there are salespeople on one side of the oven. Close the door. Hit the start button and place your bets on the grapes. Thanks to the physics of heat transfer, they will start skating across the hot oil. Some high achievers will skate fast and far. Unfortunately, the same physics of heat transfer will eventually make the grapes explode.

When people are motivated by making a gain, they will be working because they want to rather than they have to. With a personal goal to achieve, they will be motivated by positive feelings. What is their goal and what is important to them about the job? To manage and lead your people effectively you need to build a dossier of the key criteria, both towards and away, of each salesperson you manage. You can find this out by talking to them. With rapport you can be explicit and ask what is important to them. You want to know so that you can work well together. When you lead people by what is important to them, they will follow.

This is why company incentive programmes rewarding high performance with holidays or gifts often do not work. Such schemes are a blanket way of trying to motivate positively. It is like offering a customer a discount, when in fact price is not important to him. He is quite happy to pay as long as the product meets his criteria. If it does not, you would be hard put giving it away.

Many incentives are simply giving people the wrong sweets. They will take them if they are the only thing on offer, but they are not really satisfying. Too much of what you do not want is never enough. There have been many research projects in industry to find out what motivates people the most and money consistently comes third or

fourth on the list. More important to a salesperson is to be acknow-
ledged, recognised and valued, and given support and guidance. To
motivate people, give them what they value. When you do, your salespeople will become more self-motivated and you will start to break out
of the vicious circle where they constantly look outside themselves, to
you, for carrots and sticks.

To motivate yourself, compare where you are now with an
inspiring future made from *your own goals and values*. To motivate
others, get them to compare where they are now with *their* vision of
an inspiring future. To judge progress, however, compare where you
are with *where you started from*.

LOGICAL LEVELS
OF MANAGEMENT

17

Imagine you are talking about a difficult account with your sales team. The account started well; it now seems to be flagging. You probe for reasons. One of the team says, 'It's a really difficult place to work in. There seems to be an air of gloom about the building. Our contacts keep changing, they cancel appointments at very short notice. We are finding it hard going.'

Compare this with another reply: 'It's just not our kind of account. We feel uncomfortable there.'

These two replies look superficially the same, but they are about two very different things. The first is about the *environment*. The team member is talking about the people and the place. The second is about the whole team's perception of themselves, their *identity*.

Consider another example. You are talking with some of your sales team about why results have tapered off. One says, 'Yes, I have been having some problems, I just keep making odd mistakes, I'm not sure why. I'm getting back into my stride now.'

Another says, 'I'm having trouble closing, I don't quite know why. That area seems to be a problem for me at the moment.'

The first person is talking about *behaviour*, isolated acts. To his mind they do not add up to anything more. The second is talking about the *skill* of closing.

These problems are at different levels and need different solutions. Individuals and organisations both experience problems and change at different levels. Identity, beliefs and values, skills or capabilities, behaviour and environment are known as *logical levels* or *neurological levels* in NLP. This model comes mainly from the research of NLP trainer and developer Robert Dilts.

Logical levels of management

Environment   This is the *where and when*, the people, places and things we work with.

Behaviour   The actions we engage in. Behaviour is what you *do*.

Capability   This covers the skills we use. Skills and capabilities are consistent behaviour over time that attains our goals. Capability answers the question *how* do you do it?

Beliefs and values   Beliefs are the ideas we act on as if they are true. They may or may not be true. We all have experiences where we thought something was true and later found this was not so. (Father Christmas comes to my mind.) However, true or not, we base our actions on them. Beliefs can be empowering, for example: 'Everyone has the resources they need or can create them.' Beliefs can also be limiting, for example: 'People are lazy and untrustworthy and need constant watching.' Values are what is important to us. Beliefs and values together answer the question *why* do you do something?

Identity   This is the deepest level and answers the question *who* are you? What sort of person are you and what is your mission in life?

Here are some examples of statements at the different levels in selling:

Identity   I am a good salesperson.

Beliefs and values   Selling is valuable and worthwhile work.

Capability   I am good at finding out the customer's need.

Behaviour   I got good rapport with my last customer.

Environment   I was distracted at the last sales meeting by the noise of the traffic outside the office.

How can you use this? By listening to what people say and being able to act on the right logical level.

You will hear what level a person is talking from by listening not only to what she says but also the way she says it.

Here is a general example – the phrase: 'I can't do that here.'

An identity statement is about the person, so it would stress the pronoun: '*I* can't do that here.'

Beliefs and values determine what is possible and important, thus 'I *can't* do that here' would express a person's doubt at a belief level.

'I can't *do* that here' suggests a particular skill or capability.

'I can't do *that* here' is about something specific.

'I can't do that *here*' is about the environment. It could be OK to do it elsewhere.

You can make changes at any logical level and there will be results throughout the organisation. The higher logical level you affect, the greater the change to both individual and organisation.

For example, salespeople may find difficulties because of poor office equipment, so simple interventions at the environment level, such as improved office facilities, help in travel and better information can be very effective. When staff take many days sick leave, it could be a question of morale or it could be the air-conditioning.

A company culture is an interesting example of something that can be both identity and environment. A salesperson may find it difficult fitting into a company culture. It is the environment for her, although an intangible one. Yet the company culture can also be thought of as the identity of the company, what makes it unique. It's 'the way we do things'. A company culture is easy to grasp intuitively yet hard to influence directly. Think of the cultural difference between Virgin Airlines and BA. They are both airlines, but there the resemblance ends. When you do influence a company culture, however, the changes are felt throughout the company, whereas a change in environment will not have the same effect.

Some salespeople seek a change in environment by changing jobs, but carry their beliefs and capabilities with them, guaranteeing the same problem will reoccur for them. Many people have limiting beliefs about selling and do not value it. Even though they may sell a product, they are reluctant to call it selling. So very few people will claim to be a salesperson at an identity level. A person's identity is strongly linked to his self concept and self-esteem.

Skills will not manifest without empowering beliefs and values to back them up. Change a belief and it has an effect through many skills and much behaviour. Change behaviour and it *may* have an effect at higher levels, but it is not very likely. Changing behaviour usually has little impact. Changing beliefs and skills and especially identity is generative, having multiple effects.

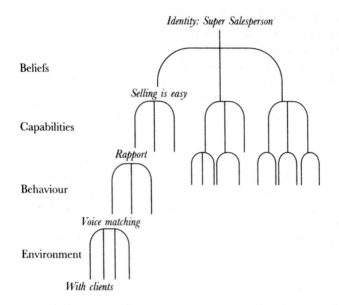

Identity: Super Salesperson

Beliefs

Selling is easy

Capabilities

Rapport

Behaviour

Voice matching

Environment

With clients

Figure 10 Logical level cascade

TRAINING

One way to use these logical levels to advantage is in training. A lot of sales training is viewed with suspicion and scepticism, and rightly so. As we have argued, a lot of motivational training is operating at the wrong level. It is a short-term bandage for a long-term malaise. Effective sales training must operate at the level of your sense of self and congruence, otherwise it is just another attempt to train external behaviour into people. It is a behaviour level remedy for a belief or even identity level problem. To be effective, sales training must address the higher levels. This is one of the fundamental areas where NLP can bring about sustainable change. NLP is not a series of hollow techniques to sell more product.

Training imparts some mixture of skills, attitudes and knowledge. Knowledge on its own is unlikely to make much difference to salespeople, who need skills and the beliefs and values to use them. Training also needs to be tied to the organisation and has to be evaluated and measured according to pre-set criteria.

Training can fail for a number of reasons. First, the wrong people may be trained. Some people are unsuited to sales and training is not going to make a great deal of difference to them. Secondly, the training may not be goal-oriented and it may be unclear what it is meant to achieve. Thirdly, there may be no measurement and evaluation of the results, either for the individual or for the organisation. The training may be good or bad, but there is no way of knowing. Lastly, there may be no support for the trainees back at the workplace. A training course may be treated as a small holiday or a necessary evil before the trainee comes back to get down to some 'real work'. Organisational training and its effects are dealt with in detail in the book *Training with NLP* (see Bibliography).

Modelling projects

'He's a born salesman.' We have heard that phrase many times. What does it mean? It cannot be literally true. It really means he is an excellent salesperson and no one (including him) knows how he does it. An explanation of inborn talent simply masks our lack of knowledge. People who are very good at what they do make it look simple, easy and natural, yet time and effort has gone into developing the skill. The finished product is like a building without the scaffolding – it looks a miraculous achievement, but could not have been built without the scaffolding. Modelling projects discover the scaffolding for these skills so others can use them to build their skills.

NLP originally developed by modelling communication and influencing skills, and today NLP modelling projects are used in education and business. For example, Robert Dilts has conducted a major research project with the multinational company Fiat to identify the skills needed for leadership, because the quality of their leaders is a key part of their organisational development strategy.

Modelling can be used in selling in a variety of ways. First, it can be used to discover the patterns used by successful salespeople, those who are not only successful at selling but who also maintain a balanced life. However you evaluate skills, there are always the star performers whose talents, if only they could be shared, would make a great difference to organisational results. The so-called Pareto Principle states that 80 per cent of the results are achieved by 20 per cent of the people in any organisation. What a waste of possibilities. We can now model from top performers how they get their results and design specific training to teach these strategies to the average performers, so that *they can all do what the best people do.*

A sales modelling project would typically involve consulting the organisation and deciding what skills are worth modelling and who the top performers are. Procedures would be set up so individual and organisational results could be measured and the project evaluated. The next step would be to spend time with the models and watch them in sales meetings, interview them and build a model of what they do that involves their beliefs and values, mental strategies, meta-programs and the logical levels they operate on. We would also want briefly to interview their managers and a few of their colleagues to get a number of different descriptions. From here we could start to build a model of what the excellent performers do. Patterns become clearer by contrast, so it would also be useful to interview and watch the average salespeople and note what is different about what *they* do. Compare and contrast the average with the outstanding.

The second stage of a modelling project is to test results. Teach the average salesperson the skills you have modelled from the top performers and see what difference this makes. Apply the measurement standards that you have already agreed to evaluate the differences. If the evaluation is positive, then the whole project can be written up and implemented throughout the company.

The last step is to design a training programme to teach the model to the whole sales force in co-operation with the organisation's trainers. A trainer's training programme is then set up, so organisational trainers can train the whole of the sales force.

The model could also be used in recruiting salespeople. Each model will be specific to the company that commissioned it because the nature of the product, the length of the sales cycle and the company culture means that one model cannot simply be grafted onto another company in the hope that it will work.

There is a broader use of modelling. You can model your own skills using NLP, so that you can apply them more widely. Often we have skills, but they seem to come and go of their own accord. NLP allows us to gain some control over our own unpredictable expertise.

Lastly, you can select role models – people who consistently manifest a way of doing business that allows them to be themselves, enables others to achieve their goals and empowers both parties to succeed and get results. Such models will have different personalities, but whoever they are, they will be true to themselves. Choose one who attracts you. You may be lucky enough to know someone like that in your organisation. We hope that others will look to you as such a model.

COACHING AND MEETINGS

COACHING

Part of sales management is coaching, that is, discussion and guidance, helping a colleague solve a problem or improve at a task. It can be formal or informal. Good coaching helps the person improve his performance. Many sales skills are used in coaching: asking good questions, eliciting what the person wants and what is important to him. When personal problems are also discussed, coaching overlaps with counselling.

A coaching session without rapport is like two cardboard cutouts with a glass panel between them, so always get rapport first. Backtracking to check agreement is also important. A coaching session should be set up with a clear agreed time frame, it should be confidential and should take place without interruption.

After rapport, the next step in a coaching session is to find out the salesperson's goals. What does he want from this session? This may well broaden out into what he wants from his work that he is not getting at the moment.

Your outcome in a coaching session is the same as at a sales meeting: to help the person achieve his goal. Use your skill at going to second position with the other person to understand his world from the inside. After the discussion, if you do not get a positive result, you can always go back to your first position and make first position business decisions.

What do you do with someone whose 'needs' are not obtainable? For example, a common scenario is the top performing salesperson who wants to be a manager and who has been turned down on a number of occasions. She now suspects that she cannot achieve a management post within the company. Her performance as a salesperson has dropped and she may be seeking a management position with a competitor. (Someone like this will be attractive to another company because of the inside knowledge she holds.) You may be the manager of someone like this and know that senior management have already decided promotion is out of the question. How do you motivate her? Find out the goal beyond the goal.

'You want to be a manager. What would having this give you?'
'Some status, both here and at home.'
'And what would having that status give you?'
'Self-respect. A sense of getting somewhere.'

You may not be able to give this person a management position. But you may be able to supply more status in a different way which would provide the self-respect and sense of progress the individual needs.

Use your knowledge of logical levels when you are coaching and motivating your salespeople. Give praise and recognition where appropriate on the identity level: '*You are* an excellent account developer.' When you give people negative feedback, give it on a behavioural level: 'It is important to gain rapport with clients before you elicit their needs. You *did not* do that with the last client. How can I help you to make sure you do it in future?' This corrects the behaviour and not the person.

The single most important idea here is to criticise the behaviour and not the identity.

Criticism

Feedback that is critical can be given in a helpful way. Its positive intention is to improve performance. Criticism needs to be factual, specific and accurate. It should be about behaviour that is under the person's control to change.

The feedback should be as soon after the event as possible. You should describe the situation as objectively as possible, give your own feelings about it, take responsibility for those feelings and then ask for the other person's views.

For example, 'Tom, at the last meeting with the clients at XYZ company, I noticed you interrupted the customer on three or four occasions. The customer became visibly annoyed. I was embarrassed and feel that what you did contributed to the poor outcome of the meeting. What do you think?'

An example of what not to do would be, 'You're an idiot. You interrupted that customer through the entire meeting and lost us that order!'

The general format for giving negative feedback is:

- Give your perceptions.
- Describe the behaviour.
- Describe the undesirable consequences.
- Ask for the criticised person's view.
- Agree a preferable future course of action and get his commitment to it.

Sloppy feedback can create resentment and does not lead to any change. One characteristic of managers who are leaders is that they can give negative feedback in such a way that the other person still feels appreciated and valued.

Be open to feedback yourself and keep yourself informed of what is happening, even the bad news. In ancient Greece, it was a common practice to have the messenger who bore bad news put to death. What happens in a culture where the messenger is blamed is that people stop becoming messengers or, if they are forced to be messengers, will only report back the good things that are happening. This provides management not with a picture of what is actually happening, but of how the messengers think the managers would like it to be. Major decisions may be taken with only half the information needed (the Hitler's bunker syndrome).

MEETINGS

Meetings can be the biggest time wasters of the day or the most productive part. Whether you are meeting with company management to determine policy, or your sales team to decide strategy or review progress, there are some principles that can save you hundreds of hours in a year.

The first rule is – do not have a meeting at all if you can achieve your goal by telephone, letter or electronic mail.

If a meeting *is* needed, settle the membership and the agenda of the meeting in advance. Limit the meeting to the people who matter and who can make decisions. If a key person or a sizeable minority of the people is missing, cancel the meeting.

Enter the meeting in a resourceful state. Use the resource anchors you have set up (see the self-management section) before you start the meeting and use them to keep you in a resourceful state if the meeting goes awry. If the sight of another person and the sound of her voice affects your state, that other person is actually a negative anchor for you. Be prepared if you have to meet such a person in the meeting. Also, have you considered what sort of anchor you are for others? What feelings does the sight of you elicit in your sales team?

Before you start the meeting, know your goal for that meeting and the evidence you want to see, hear and feel that will tell you you have it. Encourage all your team to set goals before the meeting. This one step alone will save many fruitless hours.

When the meeting starts, get consensus on one or a number of shared outcomes for the meeting and a time frame. Make it clear the meeting will end on time. Write the shared goal of the meeting on a flip chart so it is in constant view. For example:

> To review the present state of the XYZ account, decide what needs to be done next and allocate those tasks.

During the meeting, use the same questioning skills you use in selling to find out what people want within the framework of the agreed goal. Use the agreed agenda to challenge any irrelevancy. Keep the meeting on track. Contributions may be interesting, informative and true and still be red herrings. If someone brings up an irrelevancy, use a challenge like this: 'That's interesting, but I don't see how it fits into our goal for this meeting.' As you say this, gesture with your hand or head in the direction of the written goal. When you do this consistently, the gesture becomes an anchor for relevancy. Once such an anchor is established, you have only to make the gesture to make the point. It is then for the speaker to show how his contribution is relevant. If it is not, but is nevertheless important, you can agree it must be discussed at another time.

At the close of the meeting, use backtracking to go over the main points and check for agreement. Use the conditional close when necessary: 'If we did X and not Y, then would that take care of the issue?' Allocate tasks and check everyone knows what they have to do. You can also future pace the decisions by exploring some of the possible consequences.

Delegation

You will probably delegate tasks during a meeting: passing responsibilities to a subordinate. When used as part of a subordinate's development or to relieve the manager's workload at times of increased pressure or as a way of supporting the team, delegation works well. When used to dump unwanted jobs onto someone who can't say 'no' so that the manager can have an easier life, delegation works badly.

When delegating, be clear about your reason for it and choose someone who will benefit most from performing the task. Explain the task and ask whether the person is willing and feels capable of doing it. Calibrate that person for any incongruity. If she says 'yes' but you perceive she is doubtful, the best move is often to discuss it in private afterwards. Ask what help might be needed and agree a method of monitoring progress with a completion date.

Whenever possible, leave it up to the subordinate to come to you at the time of completion. This gives an extra sense of control and responsibility. Never say, 'Let me know if you get into trouble.' People tend not to report back failure. If the task is important and you feel you must be kept informed of progress, agree reported updates at the time of delegation. Otherwise your interest will be received as interference and the task will seem only half delegated, the responsibility without the authority.

Joint Visits

Attending sales calls with salespeople is one of the most important functions in sales management. Unfortunately it is an aspect of the job that many people choose to forget. In a reactive environment, a joint visit is one of the easiest tasks to postpone to make room for something else. It's easy to promise to go on another one soon, but joint visits should be treated as a priority, planned in the diary and cancelled only as a last resort, when no other option is open.

The frequency of joint visits will be influenced by your industry and geography. The important thing is to see them as a major part of management and not a gap filler.

There are a number of reasons for going on joint visits:

- To help close a piece of business when the salesperson feels extra status will make a difference or where she simply wants a second opinion on how to handle it.
- To observe a salesperson's performance so you can both identify areas of improvement as part of a development plan.
- To have contact with a salesperson away from the office in order to

build on your relationship.
- To maintain your own contact with the market-place.
- To observe methods of operation in order to cross-fertilise with the rest of the team.

Whatever your goal, let the salesperson know, otherwise your presence may be interpreted as 'checking up'.

When you have agreed an outcome for your time with the salesperson, plan the call itself. Allow the salesperson to take the lead in the planning process; it is her call. Establish an outcome and a method of conducting the call. Ask for background to the meeting, where the customer and salesperson are in the sales process. What will be the evidence that they have achieved what they are planning to achieve? What contingency plans are there? And, most importantly, what does the salesperson want you to do when you are in the customer's office? It is important that the salesperson specifies your behaviour and that you stick to it. If your outcome is to identify skill strengths and weaknesses, it is pointless for you take centre stage and say, 'Pleased to meet you. I'm the manager. I'll be doing most of the talking.' If you do not agree on your behaviour, you may well find the salesperson sitting back expecting you to take control.

After the joint visit, you should review what took place. Although your observations are important, they are secondary to the salesperson's assessment of what happened. Wait until he speaks. Most salespeople will wallow in the opportunity to point out every tiny mistake they made. Ask questions that focus on the positives and use the time to coach.

Give a mixture of feedback and make it very specific. It is best to start with positive feedback, for example, 'Dave, I really liked the way you dealt with that point about pricing policy. Referring to minimum quality specifications and customer feedback answered the point and reassured the customer at the same time.'

Then give the negative if there is any. Always ask the salesperson what he could have done differently and, if he is uncertain, suggest an alternative. For example, 'I thought your closing was rather weak. You could have used the conditional close on delivery and got a minimum commitment.'

Support the salesperson to identify the learning points. Ask him how he will do things differently next time. The purpose of the review is to help the salesperson improve and feel good about the future.

ORGANISATIONAL DEVELOPMENT AND LEARNING

Change and stability

Management has to keep an organisation running and improve the business. Keeping running is about doing the same thing. Improvement is about change. So how do you balance the two? Attempting both at the same time, at the same logical level, can feel like running on the spot while trying to go forward.

Keeping a sales organisation running during times of change requires the management of the sales pipeline. You need to manage, set targets, monitor progress and ensure activity for every step in the sales cycle, constantly. If you succumb to short-term pressure to place emphasis on closing sales earlier than would normally happen to the detriment of contacting new prospects, presenting or demonstrating to warm contacts, you will find yourself on a downward spiral to total reactivity.

Different products and markets have different sales cycles and, therefore, different pipeline requirements. You need to measure the length of the average sales cycle and the drop off rates of each of the steps along the way so you can backward plan. Whatever the length of the sales cycle, you have to make sure the different sorts of sales activity are spread evenly to avoid one of the greatest sales headaches – peaks and troughs in results.

Change is hard to introduce and manage in a company because any organisation is a system where all the pieces are connected. Like many medicines, change can have side-effects, often unforeseen, on parts of the body not even connected to the original ailing part. So a manager must think of the long-term consequences of whatever he does and to do this he needs a time line that has a representation of the far future. Yet in order to deal day to day, a manager needs a representation of the immediate future. If, as a manager, you have a tendency to either 'in time' or 'through time' thinking, you must manage yourself in order to cover both forms of thinking.

A fair system of rewards

Organisational structures have a big influence on individual results. An individual is not always in total control of the factors that influence performance. Consequently, many leaders in the Total Quality Management (TQM) field, notably Edwards Deming, argue that commission-based rewards are unfair. How can we distinguish between systemic effects and true individual differences? It is almost unmeasurable.

Thinking systemically, positive intentions may have unintended side-effects. Paying salespeople commission can cause them to push products a customer does not need or to ignore small clients and concentrate on the large ones. Neither of these results is in the company's interests and nor likely to have been part of the intention to motivate.

As the New Bazaar develops, it is quite likely that commission-based selling will die out and new systems will take its place. This is already happening in some industries.

How else can you reward people? Many organisations are wrestling with this problem. Management and employee perception of a compensation system is bound to differ. After all, there can be no such thing as an objective evaluation system. (Objective from whose viewpoint anyway?) Merit-based pay needs some sort of evaluation system. An evaluation system needs standards and criteria. But against whose values do you set them?

THE LEARNING ORGANISATION

Organisational change happens at a high logical level. The form of change often comes from a few critical individuals making decisions based on differing values. However, a company does not improve its results unless it is open to change and learning.

A learning organisation recognises the importance of the people within it, supports their full development, and creates a context in which they can learn and become leaders. A learning organisation is a 'know' organisation and not a 'no' organisation.

Peter Senge, director of the systems thinking and organisational learning programme at the Sloan School of Management,

Massachusetts Institute of Technology (MIT), writes about the art and practice of the learning organisation in his fine book *The Fifth Discipline* (see Bibliography). He identifies five key disciplines that are needed to create a learning organisation. The first is building shared vision by creating a set of goals and values that inspire and motivate all of the members of the organisation. The second, team learning, is how people form effective teams. The third he calls 'mental models': the unconscious ideas of individuals and groups that shape their behaviour and decisions. In this book we have called these ideas beliefs and values. Fourth, there is personal mastery: a lifelong commitment to improving skills.

The fifth discipline of the title is systemic thinking. This type of thinking sees the interconnection of events rather than linear cause and effect, and how the consequences of management decisions show up in unexpected ways in the future, far apart in space and time from the original decision. Sometimes we do not learn from experience because we do not connect cause with the experience itself. The time gap is too long. Systemic thinking can show how a company structure can create problems and how the consequences of executive decisions show up elsewhere in the system, coming back to create the very problem they were designed to alleviate.

An example is how motivational training can disempower salespeople by encouraging them to rely on outside motivation and distancing them from their own values and goals. The more of this type of training you get the more of it you need. It is iatrogenic medicine: a medicine that fosters the condition it purports to cure.

MANAGING CHANGE

Enough theory. What can you do as a manager to create an empowering environment for yourself and others?

We have already talked about managing by values, recognising and valuing each salesperson. You can prime people to be self-directed, they will pick up your proactive style and the more they do this the less you need to manage them. Transfer knowledge equally, share ideas through dialogue and discussion. Be open to feedback and willing to take different viewpoints.

Reframe mistakes as progress and learning experiences that are essential to progress. The exemplary example is the story of the salesman in a large computer company who was handling a very large account. He took it almost to completion, then made a glaring error, forgot some key information and lost the sale. His mistakes cost the company several thousand pounds. His manager called him into the office.

'I suppose you are going to fire me,' he said.

'Of course not,' said his manager. 'We have just invested several thousand pounds on your impromptu training. Make the same mistake again and we will fire you.'

In any organisation there will be a balance between task and relationship. Good relationships support good work. One sales manager of a small manufacturing company was concerned about the poor relationships between members of his team. They rarely got together, never seemed to share their experiences and were becoming isolated. Results were falling off. He made a very simple move at the environmental level. He bought a refrigerator out of office funds and installed it in a corner of the office. The refrigerator soon became a focus where people made cups of coffee and got talking to share gossip. A month later the refrigerator was an established meeting-place. The office atmosphere improved. Morale started to climb. Results improved. The manager was able to fend off attempts by higher management to take away the refrigerator because they thought 'salespeople were standing round all day gossiping instead of doing any work'...

It is not easy to introduce New Bazaar type of management if the workplace has been dominated by external, 'away from', 'Attila the Hun' management intent on frightening their sales team into selling quantity regardless of need. It cannot be done all at once. Pace the current reality before leading. People have to feel safe before they will follow. This is not an ideal world and the bottom line for business is results. To influence higher management you need good results.

How do you do it? You use exactly the same influencing skills as you use to manage your sales team, only your goal is different. Affirm your own manager's identity and put your ideas for behaviour level change that will get better results. Know the values of the people you want to influence. Become the person who delivers good results so you are an anchor for good news. Create rapport and build alliances to create a situation where you both win.

The management model in the New Bazaar is leadership based on empowering beliefs and values. NLP communication, influencing and modelling skills give the means to bring this about. We, the authors, are practical idealists. We would not be arguing these models and this approach, writing, training and consulting, unless we were congruent ourselves that they work and had seen them working.

There is a saying in NLP: 'If you always do what you've always done, you'll always get what you've always got.' We hope that we have argued the disadvantages of the Old Bazaar and the value of the New Bazaar sufficiently cogently for you to consider the change worthwhile.

PART FIVE

ACTION

SKILLS FOR THE NEW BAZAAR

If the ideas in this book interest you, you are probably keen to put them into practice. Here is a series of practical exercises to help you do this. Some are directly concerned with sales, others indirectly. All aim to build the skills covered in the preceding pages.

We suggest you use all these exercises. Some will be easy, others more testing. We suggest you follow the given sequence first. Start from where you are, your present state. Progress at your own pace. At a comfortable rate, the exercises will take you between a month and six weeks. There are no 'right' or 'wrong' ways to do these exercises. Simply notice the results you get. Keep a brief record of your progress and results.

You can construct a balanced programme of the skills you enjoy, the ones you want to go more deeply into and the ones that give you the best results. You can combine exercises together if you wish. There are suggestions about how to do this.

Some of these exercises are used in our sales training. Some need more practice and persistence than others, and the support a training gives can make a difference. If you are interested in our sales trainings, see the Consultancy section at the back of this book for details.

CAUTION

Wherever possible, first practise these skills in a social situation with friends and colleagues. Only use them with customers when you feel confident and comfortable about them.

Enjoy these exercises. We would be pleased to receive your feedback about them.

I. YOUR PRESENT SITUATION

This first section is to show you where you are starting from, to explore what you want and what is important to you.

If you do not know where you are starting from it is hard to plot your course to a desired future. If you do not know what you want, you will never get it.

1. **Do the small experiment on page 128 if you have not already done so. Without thinking at length, complete the following sentences:**

> Selling is like…
> Then I am…
> I would like selling to be like…
> Then I would be…

2. **List up to 10 features of your job you really like.**

> Now use money as a measure of the value you place on them.
> Ask yourself, 'If I had to give up [feature] in my work, how much extra salary would I want as compensation?'
> Put a figure beside each of your chosen features. This will give you a guide to what is important to you about your present work.
> Add up the total.
> Now list up to 10 features of your work you would like to change.
> Ask yourself, 'What extra salary would I want as compensation if these features will always be there?'
> This gives you a guide to your 'away from' values about your present work.
> Add up the total.
> If the first total is greater than the second total, you perceive the benefits as outweighing the disadvantages.
> If the first total is less than the second total, you perceive the disadvantages as outweighing the benefits.

3. **Discover how you organise time – your time line (see page 46):**

> Think of something you did in the distant past.
> Think of something you did yesterday.
> Which direction do these come from?
>
> Think of something you plan to do tomorrow.
> Think of your long-term plans for the future.

Which direction do these come from?
Notice how the memories of the past are connected to the plans for the future by a line. This is your time line.

Where do you experience 'now'?
If it is in front of you, you are a 'through time' person.
If it is inside your body you are an 'in time' person.

4. Do the exercise on page 132 to explore your main professional goal.
Pay particular attention to:

The resources you have or can create.
The evidence you need to let you know you have achieved it.
The wider consequences in your life of achieving it.

5. Do the exercise on page 141 to explore your six main professional values.

Rank them in order.
What are your rules for their achievement?

2. YOUR PRODUCT

These questions are designed for you to know your product as well as possible, in order that you can be congruent that it fits the customer's need.

1. Make a list of the most difficult questions you could be asked about your product and think of answers that satisfy you.

2. Think about your product or service and list its features and advantages:

> What problems does it solve?
> Who are the people most likely to have those problems?
> Who would never use your product?
> What else would have to be true about a person to have a need for the product?
> What other products would he have to have?
> What other problems could it solve?
> If our current market-place disappeared, how could you stop going out of business?

3. Produce your ideal customer profile (see page 56).
   Produce your problem customer profile (see page 56).

4. Write a description of your product:

> using mostly visual words
> using mostly auditory words
> using mostly kinesthetic (feeling) words

Be able to describe the product in any of these ways, or a mixture of all three.

5. Make a list of the good points of similarity of your product with others on the market.
   Then make a list of how your product differs from those on the market.
   Know both lists in order that you can give both views to customers.

3. THE TELEPHONE

These exercises will make sure you get good telephone rapport. They also give you the skills you need to pace and lead an angry or difficult caller into a more reasonable frame of mind (see page 69). This section also introduces voice matching so you may build rapport easily when face to face with customers.

1. Start to notice how people's voices change when they are talking to different people on the telephone. See if you can guess who they are talking to by their voice.

2. Experiment by matching the general voice volume of the people you talk to on the telephone. Notice whether the calls flow more smoothly. Notice how easy this is for you.

   When you feel comfortable matching, pick an easy call and, once you have rapport, start to lower the volume of your voice. Notice whether your telephone partner follows. If he does, you have good rapport, and you have paced his voice and then been able to lead. If he does not, go back to pacing.

3. Experiment by matching speed of speech. When you feel comfortable, pick a call and endeavour to lead your partner to a slower rhythm by slowing your own voice.

4. Match volume and speed at the same time. Once you have matched, pace and lead the caller to a slower, softer tonality (or a louder, faster one if you prefer).

5. Experiment by mismatching volume and speed at the end of a call. Decide when you want the conversation to end and speed up your voice and speak slightly louder. Listen to whether the other person follows and terminates the conversation. If he does not, then you can use words like 'I must be going now, speak to you later…' etc.

6. Keep records of your telephone work for a week (see page 67).

4. ORGANISING YOUR WORK

Do the exercise on page 39 for one week.

From a through time line:
  set goals
  prioritise
  divide into tasks

5. RAPPORT

Rapport is one of the most important skills in the New Bazaar. The level of your rapport skill is a direct reflection of the level of your sales success.

Start these exercises in situations where you feel comfortable. Do not use them with customers until you feel ready. You may feel self-conscious at first. This is because you are becoming aware of skills that are normally unconscious in order to improve them – just as in sport, a coach would analyse and make you aware of what you do already in order for you to become better.

Remember that rapport skills are hollow unless you are interested in the other person. They flow from your desire to establish a connection.

Body language

1. **Notice those of your colleagues who have good rapport skills. What do they do? Ask them what they think they do to get on well with customers. Does what they describe match what you have observed?**

2. **Notice the body language of colleagues as they talk in meetings and general conversation. Do they match body language? Observe strangers talking. Go 'people watching'. Do you see people matching body language? Could you tell which people are getting on well in their conversation just by observing their body language, without hearing their words?**

   Start to respectfully match general posture and speed of gesture with friends and colleagues. Notice any difference this makes to the conversation. You can also experiment and mismatch these two aspects of body language. Notice whether this makes a difference to the flow of the conversation. (Caution: This can make people very uncomfortable if you persist. Go back to matching afterwards.)

3. **Match the amount of eye contact used by colleagues and customers. If they give a lot of eye contact, give a lot in return. If they are sparing, be sparing too.**

Voice tone

When you are comfortable matching voice tone from telephone conversations, match volume and speed of voice with friends and colleagues in face-to-face conversations. When you are confident, begin to voice match with selected customers in face-to-face meetings. Notice the results you get.

Speaking the customer's language

The purpose of these next exercises is threefold:

1. To find out your own preferred ways of thinking and speaking: what you do naturally.

2. To sensitise you to the way your customer speaks and thinks.

3. To be able to respond to the customer in his preferred way to create rapport and understanding.

You will be talking in the customer's language. He will understand you and then respond to you more readily.

Being aware of predicates

1. See the exercise on page 85 on becoming aware of your own preferred speech patterns.

Talk for about five minutes into a tape recorder about your work and then play it back. Notice the predicates you use. Is it an equal mixture, or do you favour one or two systems? If you favour one system you will get good rapport and be able to influence those customers who use the same system as you. You will have less influence with customers who favour another system.

Listening for predicates

2. During the course of a day, listen carefully to one person, a friend or colleague, and notice which sort of predicate she uses. Does she use visual words, hearing words or feeling/action words the most?

Responding with predicates

3. In a conversation with a friend or colleague, notice which predicate he uses and respond with one from the same representational system. For example;

| Colleague: | 'I see the Jones account is *looking* up.' |
| You: | 'Yes, a *bright* future there I hope.' |

Keep your replies simple to start with. Once you have matched the predicate, forget about matching for the rest of the conversation if you wish.

Eye movements

(Refer to page 101.)

These exercises are to help you become aware of the subtle eye movements that people make as they think. Once you see them they become obvious.

You will use these to find out how customers are thinking and be able to tune your words and proposal in the way they find easiest to appreciate. Noticing eye movements is also part of calibration – seeing the individual non-verbal signals that indicate certain states such as interest, boredom, readiness to buy, etc.

1. Watch people on television interviews. Watch particularly when they are asked a question. What eye movements are they making? What are the eye movements they favour? Can you find any link between an eye movement and the words they say? For example, do they look down and to their right when they are experiencing an emotion or just before talking about a feeling? Do they look up or defocus before describing something they have seen?

2. Ask a friend or colleague to describe something (a holiday, a meeting) and watch his eye movements. Can you see a connection between his eye movements and what he is describing?

3. When you are comfortable with your ability to notice eye movements, have a conversation with your colleague or friend. When he makes a visual eye movement, put a visual word or phrase in your next reply. Visual eye movements are usually easiest to see. When you are ready, apply the same principles to auditory eye movements and then feeling eye movements.

4. When you are comfortable about doing this with friends and colleagues, start to notice customers' eye movements. Respond with predicates that link with that eye movement.

6. CUSTOMERS' GOALS, VALUES AND DECISIONS

1. Listen to your customers as they describe their need. Are they predominantly moving away from a problem or towards a solution?

2. Use the key questions to elicit customer's criteria and rules, if you do not do so already (see page 95).

    What do you want in a...?
    What does ... mean to you?

3. Find out the customer's decision strategy by asking, *'How will you decide whether ... is for you?'*
    Notice the answer you get. It is likely to be one of the following:

    'It looks right.'
    'It sounds right.'
    'It feels right.'
    'It makes sense.'

4. Discover the customer's buying strategy by asking, *'How did you buy your last...?'*

5. After each meeting make a short note of:

    What the customer is moving away from.
    What the customer wants to achieve.
    Which of these two was more important.
    What are the important criteria your product needs to meet.
    The rules for these criteria to be fulfilled.

7. BACKTRACKING

(See page 77.)

1. Ask a friend or colleague to describe a pleasant experience. Notice the important marked out words that she uses. Tell her what you are doing. Make it a game. Say you are going to describe her experience back to them in two different ways, and you want to know which way she prefers.

   First, play the experience back to her but substitute your own words for her important words. Then backtrack what she said, using her key words. Ask her which description she prefers.

2. When you feel ready, listen and watch for the words the customer uses when describing his values and rules.

   Backtrack those values and rules, using exactly the same words. Notice whether this enhances rapport.

8. DIFFERENT VIEWPOINTS

1. Think back to a particular sale you are proud of. Imagine the sale again in your mind's eye from your own point of view. See the customer again as best you can. Rehear some of the things she said as best you can.

   Now imagine how the sale looked from the customer's point of view. Imagine looking at yourself from the customer's perspective, hearing your voice and responding to that voice as the customer.

   Now imagine yourself outside the sale in a position where you can see both yourself and the customer talking. Hear both voices.

   > Which one of these points of view was easiest?
   > Which one was hardest?

2. Pick one friend or colleague every day and for a small part of that time with him imagine what it is like from his perspective. How is he feeling? What does he want?

   Then be aware of your own position. How are you feeling? What do you want?

   Then take a detached view. How are you relating to each other?

3. When you feel confident do this with a customer. How is he feeling? What does he want?

   Then be aware of your own position. How are you feeling? What do you want?

   Then take a detached view. Is there a match between what the customer needs and the product or service?

9. MEETINGS

1. Set up a resource anchor for yourself that you can use in any meeting (see page 157).

2. Use the meeting preparation plan (see page 154).

3. Mentally debrief after that meeting (see page 159). What did you learn from that meeting? Did you get more from it than you usually do?

10. CONGRUENCE

Finally, some ways of exploring congruence, your own alignment and balance within yourself. This is your strongest personal quality as a salesperson.

1. Take a few minutes to look back on some times in your life, both personal and professional, where you were outstandingly effective and felt truly yourself. What are the main characteristics of those times?

2. Mentally take stock of all your strengths and resources as a professional salesperson, all those things about yourself that you want to increase to build your ideal professional self-image.

   In the same way, take stock and acknowledge all those things about yourself that no longer fit into your professional self-image, and whether you would change them now or not.

3. If you had to summarise your mission in one sentence, what would it be?

4. Set up your congruency signal (see page 153 for a description of the process). Use it before selected sales meetings to check you are well prepared.

PROFESSIONAL ALIGNMENT EXERCISE

Here is a final powerful exercise to build your resources and your congruence. It will take you through the NLP logical levels. You can think it through, but it is more powerful if you can physically move forward step by step and we will describe the process in this way.

You are going to move physically forward as a way of exploring different parts of yourself. Do this exercise in a place where you can be alone and undisturbed for about 10 minutes.

- **Start by standing where you can take five steps forward. Think of your sales environment. You may think of the office you are based in or of being with your clients. Where are you? Who is around you? What products and literature do you have? When do you work and for how long?**

- **Take a step forward. This is the next level where you can explore your behaviour. What are you actually doing? Think about your movements, actions and thoughts.**

- **Take a step forward. Consider how what you do builds into your sales skills. What skills do you have? Think of your skills of rapport, questioning and needs analysis. What capabilities do you bring to this situation? Skills are simply actions that are consistent, over time, that get you the outcomes you want from them.**

- **Step forward again and reflect on your beliefs and values about selling. Why do you sell? Here are some questions to focus you on this area:**

  Does selling get you what you want?
  What do you believe about yourself as a salesperson?
  What do you believe about your customers?
  What might get in the way of you being the best salesperson you can be?
  What is 'good' selling all about?
  What do you find worthwhile about selling?
  What would you have to give up if you stopped selling?
  What is important to you about selling?
  What do you believe about the products you sell?

Take the time you need to come to answers that satisfy you.

- You are not what you do or even what you believe. Step forward again and think about your unique personality and identity.

    What is your mission in life?
    How does selling connect to it?
    Who are you?

    Get a sense of yourself and what you want to accomplish in the world. If there was one great work you could do in this life, what would it be?

- Now take a last step forward. Think about how you are connected to all other living beings and whatever you believe is beyond your life. Many people call this the spiritual realm. You may have religious beliefs or a personal philosophy. Take the time you need to get a sense of what this means to you. At the very least this is about how you, as a unique person, connect with others.

- Still feeling this connectedness with others, turn around and face back the way you came. Take this sense of connectedness with you as you step back into your identity level. Notice the difference this makes.

- Now take this enhanced sense of who you are and who you can be, and step back to your beliefs and values. What is important now? What do you believe now? What do you want to be important? What do you want to believe? What beliefs and values express your identity?

- Take this new sense and step back to the skill level. How are your skills transformed and deepened? How can you use your skills in the best possible way? How can you act to express the alignment you feel?

- Step to the behaviour level. How will this sense of self manifest in what you do?

- Finally, step back into your sales environment. How is it different when you bring these levels of your self into it? Sometimes we are stuck at the environmental and behavioural level, doing the same things, with the same people, in the same places. You are more than this. Notice how differently you feel about where you are with this greater depth and clarity from your values, purpose and sense of connectedness.

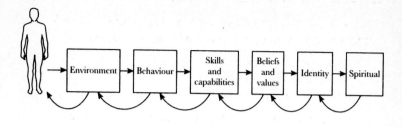

Figure 11 Logical level selling

PART SIX

RESOURCES

BIBLIOGRAPHY

Aspromonte, Don, and Austin, Diane, *Green Light Selling*, Cahill Mountain Press, 1990.

Covey, Stephen, *The Seven Habits of Highly Effective People*, Simon & Schuster Ltd, 1989

Drozdeck, Steven, Yeager, Joseph, and Sommer, Linda, *What They Don't Teach You In Sales 101*, McGraw-Hill, 1991.

Fisher, Roger, and Ury, William, *Getting to Yes*, Arrow, 1987.

James, Tad, *TimeLine Therapy and the Basis of Personality*, MetaPublications, 1988.

Johnson, Spencer, and Wilson, Larry, *The One Minute Salesperson*, Fontana, 1986.

Kline, Peter, and Saunders, Bernard, *Ten Steps to a Learning Organisation*, Great Ocean Publishers, 1993.

Laborde, Genie, *Influencing with Integrity*, Syntony Publishing Co., 1984.

Morgan, Sharon Drew, *Sales on the Line*, Metamorphous Press, 1993.

O'Connor, Joseph, and Seymour, John, *Introducing Neuro-Linguistic Programming*, Aquarian, 1993 (revised).

—, *Training with NLP*, Thorsons, 1994.

O'Connor, Joseph, and McDermott, Ian, *Principles of NLP*, Thorsons, forthcoming 1996

Robertson, James, *Sales: The Mind's Side*, Metamorphous Press 1990.

Senge, Peter, *The Fifth Discipline*, Century Business, 1990.

GLOSSARY OF TERMS

NLP AND SALES

Anchor Any stimulus that is associated with a particular response. Anchors can happen naturally; for example, the national anthem or a red traffic light. They can also be set up intentionally; for example, you can associate a phrase or gesture to a product benefit.

Anchoring Making an association between a stimulus and a response.

Associated Being inside an experience, seeing it through your own eyes and experiencing it fully.

Auditory To do with the sense of hearing.

Backtracking Restating the key points using the customer's own words. A very important sales skill for summarising, maintaining rapport and gaining commitment.

Behaviour In NLP used to describe the actions we do. It includes thought processes. Behaviour is also one of the logical levels.

Beliefs The generalisations that we make about ourselves, others and the world. Beliefs act as self-fulfilling prophecies that influence all our behaviour. One of the logical levels.

Blame frame Giving others control and responsibility for what happens, so if events go wrong, they are at fault.

Body language The largest channel of communication – includes your dress, grooming, posture, gestures and movements.

Calibrating Accurately recognising another person's internal state by reading non-verbal external signals; for example, calibrating to the customer's signals of interest.

Capability	A skill, a consistent successful strategy for carrying out a task. One of the logical levels.
Chunking	Changing perceptions by moving up or down levels. Chunking up is going up and looking at a level that includes what you are studying; for example, what need your product is a solution to. Chunking down is going down a level to look at a more specific example or part of what you are studying; for example, different versions of your product to meet the customer's need.
Conditional close	Closing a sale or transaction providing certain conditions are met. It takes the form of, 'If [condition] were met, then would we have an agreement?'
Congruence	This is when all parts of your communication are consistently giving the same message. This includes behaviour, words, tonality and body language – 'walking your talk'. It is also when all parts of you are working together towards a goal or outcome.
Criteria	What is important to you in a particular context, how you apply a value.
Criterial equivalents	The events that have to happen for criteria to be met, the rules for their fulfilment.
Cross over matching	Matching a person's body language with a different type of movement, for example, moving your hand in time with her rhythm of speech.
Decision strategy	How a customer decides to buy, the sequence of thoughts and feelings he experiences.
Electronic Bazaar	Using technology to match customer and product, without a live salesperson.
Eliciting	The skill of drawing out behaviour from others, including comments, questions, outcomes, states, skills and capabilities. Can be done verbally or non-verbally.
Emotional state	Also called simply 'state' or 'internal state'. It is a complex of all our thoughts and feelings, and we are usually aware of it as a dominant emotion.
Environment	The places, people, things, atmosphere outside yourself. One of the logical levels.
External behaviour	What you do and say, expressing your internal state.

Eye movements	The movements that correspond with how we are thinking or what representation system we are using; visual, auditory or kinesthetic. Sometimes called 'lateral eye movements' (LEM) or 'eye accessing cues'.
First position	Experiencing the world from your own point of view and being in touch with your own reality. One of the three perceptual positions, the others being second position and third position.
Future pacing	Mental rehearsal – imagining doing something or having a product in a desired future setting.
Goals	The results you want and have planned for. Also called 'outcomes' or 'objectives'. In NLP a goal needs to be stated in the positive, specifies the person's own part in achieving it, is specific enough to have sensory-based evidence and has been checked for unforeseen consequences.
Identity	Self-image or self-concept. Who people take themselves to be. One of the logical levels.
In time	Being associated in the 'now' on your time line.
Incongruence	A state of having considerations or doubts which may be conscious or unconscious. The internal conflict will be expressed in external behaviour.
Influence	Our words and actions inevitably affect others. Influence is using them to get a win–win in the present. It can be premeditated or spontaneous. It is universal and is the purpose of any interaction.
Internal dialogue	Talking to yourself, without audibly voicing the words.
Internal representations	All our thoughts and feelings. The mental pictures, sounds and feelings we remember and create.
Internal state	*see* Emotional state.
Kinesthetic	The feeling sense, including touch, emotions and the sense of balance.
Leading	Changing your own behaviour with enough rapport for the other person to follow.
Logical levels	Also known as the 'neurological levels of experience': environment, behaviour, capability, belief and identity.
Lose–lose	Any situation where neither party gains their outcome

or has their values fulfilled.

Lose–win   A situation where the salesperson makes a concession to the customer that benefits the customer and not the salesperson. Usually deteriorates into a lose–lose unless handled very carefully.

Manipulation   Manipulation is the attempt to produce an outcome that the other person perceives to be at his expense either during or shortly after the interaction. Manipulation produces a win–lose result in the short term. In the long term it is lose–lose.

Matching   Adopting some aspects of another person's communication style for the purpose of building rapport; for example, matching her posture. Matching is not mimicry, which is conscious exact copying of another person's behaviour.

Metaphor   Indirect communication by a story or figure of speech implying a comparison.

Metaprograms   Habitual and systematic filters we put on our experience, typically unconscious; for example, being motivated by moving towards rewards, rather than away from unpleasant consequences.

Mismatching   Adopting different patterns of behaviour to another person in order to redirect a meeting or conversation.

Modal operators   A linguistic term for rules or possibilities. 'Can', 'cannot', 'must', 'must not', 'ought' and 'ought not' are all modal operators.

Modelling   In NLP, used for the process of discovering the thoughts and actions that enable someone to perform a skill or task. Modelling is the basis of both NLP and accelerated learning.

Negotiation   The skill of trading off differences to reach a win–win agreement for both parties.

Neuro-Linguistic Programming   The study of excellence and a model of how individuals structure their experience.

Neurological levels   *see* Logical levels.

New Bazaar   A sales culture dominated by relationship, integrity and influence for a win–win result.

Objective	*see* Goal.
Old Bazaar	Sales culture where the sales profession is undervalued and selling is perceived as manipulative.
Outcome	*see* Goal.
Outframing	To give a situation or event a meaning that deals with certain objections in advance; for example a product is priced higher than competitors to fund research and development and maintain a high level of customer service.
Pacing	Broadly, joining others in their reality and building rapport before starting to lead somewhere different. You can pace at any level from behaviour to values and beliefs.
Perceptual position	The viewpoint we are aware of at any moment. It can be our own (first position), someone else's (second position) or an objective observer's (third position).
Positive intention	The positive purpose underlying any behaviour is what it gets for the person who does it that is important to him in his reality.
Predicates	Sensory-based words that indicate the use of a particular representational system.
Presupposition	Something that has to be taken for granted for a behaviour or statement to make sense.
Proactive	Initiating action. A metaprogram distinction.
Rapport	The process of building and maintaining a relationship of mutual trust and understanding. The basis of influence. Rapport can operate at the levels of words, non-verbal behaviour, values and beliefs.
Reactive	Responding to events rather than initiating them. A metaprogram distinction.
Reframing	Changing the way of understanding a statement or behaviour to give it another meaning.
Relevancy challenge	Asking how a specific statement or behaviour is helping to achieve an agreed outcome.
Representation systems	Internal senses, the ways we think. In NLP there are five main representational systems: visual, auditory, kinesthetic, olfactory (smell) and gustatory (taste).

Resource anchoring	The process for bringing resourceful feelings into the present moment.
Resourceful states	A combination of thoughts, feelings and physiology that makes any task easier and more enjoyable.
Second position	Seeing the world from another person's point of view and so understanding their reality. One of three perceptual positions.
Self-talk	*see* Internal dialogue.
Softeners	A gentle way of asking a delicate question. For instance, 'Would you be willing to tell me X?' rather than, 'Tell me X.'
State	*see* Emotional state.
Submodalities	The qualities of mental pictures, sounds and feelings; for example, pictures may be large or small, moving or still, in colour or black and white.
Third Position	One of the perceptual positions, perceiving the world from the viewpoint of a detached observer.
Through time	Being outside the 'now' on your time line.
Time Line	The way we subjectively represent time as a line running from past to future. A person may be 'in time', when he is in the 'now' and the line passes through his body, or 'through time', where the 'now' on the line is experienced as outside his body.
Values	The states that are important to us. Either those states we seek ('towards' values) or those we avoid ('away from' values).
Visual	To do with the sense of sight.
Voice quality	The second most important channel of communication and influence in presentations.
Win–lose	Any situation where the salesperson gets her goal and something of value, and the customer does not. The basis of manipulation.
Win–win	A situation where both parties gain something they value. *See also* win–lose, lose–lose and lose–win. Any sale that is not a win–win will become a lose–lose in the long term.

Words in bold type are in the glossary.

BUSINESS CONSULTANCY SERVICES

Joseph O'Connor and Robin Prior are available as business consultants, jointly and independently. They also work closely with Ian McDermott and International Teaching Seminars to provide a wide range of training and consultancy for:

- business communication
- organisational change
- effective and congruent selling
- organisational leadership

Modelling projects

Modelling projects are offered:

to identify and model top performers in any business area, including selling and sales management, to discover what it is that makes them excel
to design training to pass on these patterns to others

Training courses

Courses available:

- Organisational leadership
- Congruent selling
- Humour in business
- Communication skills training
- NLP certification courses

Our courses are run publicly or in house.

Software

Software is available that elicits and clarifies outcomes. The software can be tailored to the user and used together with live training.

Purpose built software offers many new possibilities for improving business processes. We design software that uses the technology in the most effective way for specific business problems and organisational development.

To find out more about any of these services contact:

Lambent Training
4 Coombe Gardens
New Malden
Surrey KT3 4AA

Telephone: +44 (0)181 715 2560
Fax: +44 (0)181 715 2560
Email: lambent@well.com
Internet: http://lambent.com

ABOUT THE AUTHORS

Joseph O'Connor is a leading author, trainer and consultant in the field of NLP, communication skills and systems thinking. He is a certified master of NLP. He has a B.Sc. Degree, and a licentiate of the Royal College of Music. His interest in sport and music has led to modelling excellent tennis players and talented musicians, and he uses this research to enrich business coaching skills.

Joseph is fascinated by individual learning and how this links to organisational learning and particularly how the Internet and purpose built computer software can make this easier.

Joseph works internationally in Europe, America and Asia. He was awarded the medal of the National Community Leadership Institute in Singapore for his work there in 1996. He was written eight books, published in thirteen languages and is interested in most things under the sun.

Other books:
Not Pulling Strings
Introducing NLP (with John Seymour)
Training with NLP (with John Seymour)
Practical NLP for Managers (with Ian McDermott)
Principles of NLP (with Ian McDermott)
NLP and Health (with Ian McDermott)
The Art of Systems Thinking (with Ian McDermott)

Videotapes:
Listening Skills in Music

Audiotapes:
An Introduction to NLP (with Ian McDermott)

Robin Prior is a business consultant, trainer, salesman, manager, writer and humorist. He is an NLP master practitioner, having been trained by John Grinder, Robert Dilts and Judith De Lozier to name but a few.

During his earlier career he sold and sales managed for companies such as Rank Xerox, British Olivetti, Pitney Bowes and GKN Sankey, where he gained an in-depth knowledge of sales training methods that were deemed at the time to be state of the art.

He has worked extensively in the financial services sector advising and training salespeople currently experiencing massive changes in legislation, customer powers and company expectations. However, his training consultancy experience embraces many industries and products. He also teaches public speaking skills, and writes speeches and corporate promotional videos.

His main objectives are to influence the world of salesmanship so that customers more often receive products that they really want and need, and salespeople live lives that are more fulfilling.

Humour being one of the great enhancers of the quality of life, Robin also writes for stand up comedians and television comedy shows.

To contact Joseph and Robin, and for further information on course, seminars and script writing, contact:

Lambent Training
4 Coombe Gardens
New Malden
Surrey KT3 4AA

Telephone: +44 (0)181 715 2560
Fax: +44 (0)181 715 2560
Email: lambent@well.com
Internet: http://lambent.com